The Mending Map

Guideposts on the Road back to Health

Copyright by Margery Phelps
© TXu-1-667-766
August 6, 2008

All rights reserved. No part of this publication may be reproduced, stored in a retrieval system, or transmitted in any form or by any means, electronic, mechanical, photocopying, recording, or otherwise, without express written permission of the copyright owner.

ISBN: 978-0-9994622-3-2

IMPORTANT NOTICE TO THE READER:

This book is for informational and general knowledge purposes of the reader only. No guarantee or assumptions are made to anyone with regard to any suggestions in this book. You are urged to contact your health professional if you are experiencing any health problems. This publication contains the opinions and ideas of the author and is sold with the understanding that the author and publisher are not engaged in rendering professional health and/or nutritional services or advice. Should the reader require advice or personal assistance with the subject matter of this publication, they are encouraged to seek the advice of a competent and licensed professional.

www.CherokeeRosePublishing.com
www.MargeryPhelps.com

Cherokee Rose
Publishing, LLC
INFORM, INSPIRE, ENTERTAIN

The Mending Map

Guideposts on the Road back to Health

Margery Phelps

Cherokee Rose Publishing, LLC

Dedication

For Andrew
with much love from
the Velcro Nana

We've met all the guides on the mending map.
Every day in every way we're doing better and better.

IMPORTANT NOTICE TO THE READER

This book is for the general knowledge and informational use of the reader only and is not intended to diagnose or treat any medical condition. No guarantees or assurances are made to anyone with regard to any suggestions in this book.

The author and publisher assume no responsibility for errors or omissions nor any liability for damages resulting from the use of information provided herein.

This book contains opinions and ideas of the author and is sold with the understanding that the publisher and author are not engaged in rendering any type of professional health or nutritional services or advice.

Should the reader require advice or personal treatments related to the subject matter of this publication, they are encouraged to seek the advice of a competent and licensed medical professional.

TABLE OF CONTENTS

INTRODUCTION i

SECTION 1: THE BODY

Chapter 1 – Find A Guide 1

Chapter 2 – Ready, Set, Go 13

Chapter 3 – Do No Harm 19

Chapter 4 – Nutrition – you are what you eat 29

Chapter 5 – It's sleepy time 41

Chapter 6 – Herbs and Supplements 47

Chapter 7 – Don't fear Alternatives 59

Chapter 8 – Physical Therapy 69

Chapter 9 – Playing it Safe 75

SECTION 2: THE MIND & EMOTIONS

Chapter 10 – Think Positive 83

Chapter 11 – Don't Despair - plateaus & setbacks 89

Chapter 12 – Let go of stress & pain 95

Chapter 13 – Affirmation, Meditation, Visualization 107

Chapter 14 – Don't play the Blame Game 119

Chapter 15 – Keep a Sense of Humor 125

Chapter 16 – PTSD, EP and EFT — let's get un-stuck 129

SECTION 3: THE SOUL

Chapter 17 – Stay in touch with your Higher Power 139

Chapter 18 – Follow your Intuition 145

Chapter 19 – Find a Hero... 151

Chapter 20 – Believe you will be well 155

SUMMARY 163

ACKNOWLEDGEMENTS 167

APPENDICES

    A.   Foods can Harm, Foods can Heal 169

    B.   Drug, Herb, and Supplement Interactions 173

    C.   Plant Chemicals that protect us 179

INDEX 181

ENDNOTES 189

OTHER BOOKS BY MARGERY PHELPS

Common Sense Medicine – a medical doctor's prescription for health care in America – Ghost writer for Robert A. Nash, MD

Harmony's House – a coloring book (for children)
Illustrations by Tonya Pash and Mike Carney

Halo's Glow (a book about healthy eating for children)
Illustrations by Aly Hopper

Mighty-Me and the Rainbow Plate (for children)
Illustrations by Julie Weinberger

You don't have to be sick – healthy eating is good medicine
With co-author, Janiece C. Andrews, MD

New Life Naturally, a home guide to harmonious health
With David Allen, Ph.D.

At First Sight – the story behind the MGM Motion Picture
Contract book for Barb and Shirl Jennings, subjects of the movie

Finding Margaret – a case for reincarnation
A narrative non-fiction

Crossing the Bridge from Life to Life
A workbook on reincarnation

Downline Dynamics – how to build a happy, healthy downline
Contract book for Janiece C. Andrews, MD

Accounting 101 for the start-up entrepreneur
A workbook on small business bookkeeping

INTRODUCTION

What is health? When I was on a lecture circuit after the publication of my first health book, one of my colleagues in the nutrition and health field opened his talks with that question. Then he would proceed to tell a graphic but amusing story:

> Three elderly men were sitting on the porch of the retirement home, sharing tales on the challenges of age. The first, and youngest, said, "What I wouldn't give for a good, satisfying stream. My poor ole bladder just dribbles."
>
> The second gentlemen chastised him. "You think that's bad. Well, I haven't had a good b.m. in so long I can't remember what it feels like to not have my bowels hurt."
>
> Then the third, and senior of the group, spoke up. "You punks just make me sick. Every morning at eight o'clock I have a good healthy stream. Then at ten o'clock sharp I have a good healthy bowel movement."
>
> He paused.... "Now, if I could just get out of bed before noon...."

Of course, the audience would roar with laughter, and the lecture would be well launched. I think there are two definitions of health:

1. <u>Health is subjective and personal</u>. It's how you feel compared to how you want to feel. For the life-long diabetic, a day with stable blood sugar could be day of good health. The cancer patient on chemo might say that he/she feels pretty darn good the day after the vomiting stops. The burn patient could relish the day he doesn't have a painful debridement, and the child with the broken arm feels great the day the cast is removed.

OR,

2. <u>Health is defined by medical tests, measuring your results against a standard</u>. A doctor would say that the diabetic is still diabetic, even during a day of normal blood sugar; the patient on chemo still has cancer, even if they feel on top of the world; burn victims have a variety of health challenges to overcome; and the child with the healed broken arm may still have calcium absorption problems.

How do you define your health? If you prefer the second definition, put this book down and read no further. I am not a health professional and therefore cannot and will not make any diagnoses or prescribe any treatments. There are thousands of advice books by doctors, PhDs, nurses, and nutritionists.

If you like the first definition, this book is for you. It is gleaned from years of personal experiences and research and what I have learned as a layperson and healthcare consumer. I'm not a health professional—I'm a journalist—but it seems to me that many people do not understand healing. When the body is injured or ill, the patient must be responsible for healing because HEALING MUST COME FROM WITHIN:

- from the body and what we feed it;
- from the mind and what we think;
- from the soul and what we believe.

All three steps are vital—like a three-legged stool—without all three true healing cannot occur. I've had a number of serious health challenges in my many years of life, and I've been told on more than one occasion that my affliction was permanent, that I'd never recover. Well, I not only recovered, I regained my health, and this book has the formulas that worked for me.

A few years back I ghost wrote a book for Robert A. Nash, M.D. entitled *Common Sense Medicine - a medical doctor's prescription for health care*. Scattered throughout the book were Doctor Bob's "Common Sense Prescriptions." Since I am not a health professional, you might say that the book you are holding is the lay-person's *Guidepost to health*. So, let's get started!

SECTION ONE

THE BODY

Chapter 1

Find a Guide

During this critical first step on the road back to health you will need to select a Guide to lead you. This *guide* should be a medical professional whom you trust and believe in – and also someone with whom you can communicate freely and openly.

The doctor you choose will not only have an immediate and direct effect on your condition, what he/she does or does not do could impact you for years, months, or even the rest of your life. For these reasons it's important to put some thought and consideration into your choice for this *partner in healing* — your personal Guide on the Mending Map.

A CASE STUDY

Believe in your doctor

My mom was having heart problems and was referred to a cardiologist. After her first appointment with him, she called me – all excited that she had a "wonderful, wonderful doctor." He scheduled her for some extensive heart exams the following week, and that weekend he was off for a family event – and wouldn't you know it, that's when my mom's heart decided it wasn't going to work anymore.

Another cardiologist was called in when she arrived at the hospital, and he did everything possible, but she remained in extremely critical condition, with little response. She was hanging on by a thread.

When her "wonderful" doctor arrived at the hospital late Sunday evening, he sat on her bed, held her hand, and told her that they were going to "get through it" and she would be fine.

Her miraculous and astonishing response was almost immediate. She sat up in bed and announced that she was hungry.

Dr. Wonderful had not done anything medically to improve my mother's condition. Her belief in him, and her faith that he would take care of her, improved her condition. She went on to have open heart surgery and made a full recovery. (More on belief in healing in Section Three.)

For those who are in a critical crisis and land in the emergency room, your ability to choose a physician may be a moot point. But hopefully a family member will have input into this decision process because it is incredibly important.

There are other constraints to your ability to choose a medical provider, and a big hurdle will be your insurance company. Your PPO or HMO will have referrals for various medical conditions, but it is still important to find a provider you trust and feel comfortable with. Since I've had so many referrals to so many specialists, I came up with my own method to qualify them:

- How friendly and accessible is their staff? Do they make you feel like you are their only patient, or do they herd you around like a Holstein on the way to the slaughterhouse?
- Did they have your paperwork (referral information) in order when you arrived or did they act like they had never heard of you?
- Were they solicitous of your condition? Did they at least try to make you comfortable?
- Were they considerate of you and your infirmities? (One time I was lost is a maze of corridors, laboratories, and exam rooms when a receptionist walked so fast I couldn't keep up with her because my foot was swollen as big as a football. I had to hobble back to the lobby and wait for her to return. And she was mad *at me* because I *didn't keep up with her*.)
- Were you kept waiting longer than thirty minutes? A well-run medical office should get you back to see the doctor within five or ten minutes. Two-hour waits are inconsiderate of the patient and indicate to me that the staff and/or doctor are scheduling more patients than they can properly handle. If the doctor has to attend to an emergency, the staff should call you and re-schedule your appointment rather than keeping you waiting endlessly when you don't feel good.

- How long were you kept waiting after you were put in an exam room? Did a nurse or physician's assistant come in right away to take your vital signs?
- Did a physician's assistant do your preliminary work-up? Was she/he thorough or did they just do a cursory exam? Did they ask you questions and engage you in a conversation?
- When the doctor came in to see you, did he introduce himself and shake your hand? Did he call you by your first name (Mary, Jim) or your surname (Mrs. Smith, Mr. Brown)?
- Did he sit down to talk to you and ask you questions, or did he just stand?
- Did he do his own exam or just review what the P.A. had already done?
- Were lab tests or x-rays ordered? Were they done on site or were you sent to an outside lab?
- Were the lab and x-ray technicians caring and considerate of your condition?
- Did they ask you questions or answer your questions?
- Did they seem over-worked or stressed?
- Were the work areas neat and organized?
- Did the doctor explain his findings and what they mean for your health in a manner that you could understand?
- Were you satisfied with the diagnosis and/or recommendations for surgery or treatments?

- Will this physician be your provider of further care, such as surgery, or were you referred to another physician? Why?
- Was the checkout procedure smooth and seamless? Did they have your insurance information on hand, and did they have your paperwork completed when you arrived at the check-out desk?
- Did the doctor tell you to schedule surgery or additional tests or x-rays? Did the check-out clerk have this paperwork for you?
- Was the appointments clerk apprised of your condition and did he/she have your medical file?
- Did they schedule the procedure right away or did they say they would call you?
- Did they tell you that they would take care of your pre-certification, which the insurance company would require?

There are no right or wrong answers to these questions; however, they should make you aware of attitudes, professionalism, and level of care the physician and his/her staff will provide. If you don't like the answers, you should seek a second opinion, or even a third if necessary.

If you have doubts about needing a second opinion remember this: Your life may depend on it. Dr. Jerome Groopman has written a book *Second Opinions* (Penguin USA, 2001). He's the expert so I defer to his judgment in this field and recommend you read his book if you want to know more about the need for a second opinion.

> ### GUIDEPOST
>
> Fear of offending the doctor is probably the main reason why patients don't get another opinion. But good doctors welcome second opinions. If your doctor doesn't, that's a red flag.
>
> Jerome Groopman, M.D.,
> Harvard Medical School
> (Quoted in AARP Bulletin, Feb. 2003)

You know those biopsies that tell you if you have cancer? A large percentage of them are wrong according to surveys at some prestigious hospitals.[1] If you receive a biopsy that has dire consequences, I can't stress enough the importance of a second opinion, or even a third if they don't agree. Take a look at these statistics:

Emory University Hospital – pathologists found that in the 14% of soft tissue samples submitted for second opinions, 45% originally diagnosed as cancer were actually benign, and 23% were cancers misdiagnosed as benign.[2]

<u>Johns Hopkins University Medical Institutions</u> – in a 21-month reanalysis of 6,000 pathology reports, 1.4% were incorrect; however, in female reproductive tract cancer, the error rate was 5.1%, and in cancers of body cavity membranes the error rate was 9.5%.[3]

<u>Miami School of Medicine</u> - 28% of liver biopsies submitted for second opinion "required a change in both diagnosis and treatment."[4]

Ernest Rosenbaum, MD, of Stanford University School of Medicine says, "The question is not why you should get a second opinion but why would you not? There is no downside," he adds.[5]

Second opinions are especially important if you have been diagnosed with a rare condition or need to know more about your treatment options. Also, according to one of my personal physicians, "older patients are more likely to be misdiagnosed," making second opinions all the more critical.

If you do want a second, or even third opinion, do yourself a favor and get your primary physician to help you. It's not a good idea to go behind your doctor's back and potentially create a more stressful situation; besides, the providers of second and third opinions will need the primary doctor's records. And please – do not go to the internet for opinions. There are too many quacks.

A CASE STUDY:

The Need for Second Opinions

I have my own reasons for suggesting you get a second opinion: I have been damaged because I did not get them and when I did, I was glad.

Several years ago, a small neuroma in my foot hurt so much I could not walk properly and as a result I injured the cartilage in my knee. I was referred to an orthopedist who recommended surgery for both the knee and foot. Although his specialty was knees, he said he could also do the foot surgery.

Not heeding that wise old inner voice that always has our best interest at heart (Intuition – Chapter 18), I went ahead with both surgeries by the knee surgeon even though I had great misgivings about the foot. Actually, I did see a foot surgeon, but he would not change his surgical schedule to accommodate the knee surgeon's schedule and I didn't want to have two separate procedures, with two separate ordeals of anesthesia.

The knee turned out great. The foot was a disaster. Afterwards, the knee man admitted he was in over his head and sent me to another orthopedic foot surgeon who recommended drastic corrective surgery which involved cutting open the bottom of my foot. This time I listened to my inner voice. Rather than having that surgery, I hobbled around for two more years.

At an appointment with my nurse practitioner, I showed her my foot; she had a hissy fit and sent me to a podiatrist who very quickly diagnosed a bone infection. Three sessions of injections and six weeks of daily doses of powerful antibiotics remedied my problem. The podiatrist also told me that he would never cut open the bottom of my foot the way the orthopedic foot surgeon had recommended.

That was not the end of my odyssey, however. A couple of years later three bones in that foot spontaneously fractured, putting me in a boot for eight months. My podiatrist said the bones were weak due to the long-term infection.

GUIDEPOST
Get a second opinion.

A CASE STUDY:

Physician's Assistants are not Doctors

There is another potential problem you should be aware of: <u>Physician's Assistants are just that: physician's assistants.</u> They are not doctors. Unfortunately, many P.A.s are treating patients and prescribing medications without proper professional oversight. This is foolish on the part of the provider and dangerous for you. Again, let me give you a personal story. If it could happen to me, it could happen to you.

I had a bad fall in the cafeteria at Turner Broadcasting where I was working. Rather than calling an ambulance, security personnel pulled me up off the floor, sat me in a chair, put some lunch in front of me and told me I'd feel better if I ate something. Not wanting to make a scene, I did as they said, even though I could not move my right arm. Wandering around in a shock-induced haze, I made my way to the Human Resources office where I was referred to Nova Care, an occupational injury provider.

At the Nova Care office on Peachtree Street in Atlanta, a short distance from TBS, a terse woman in a white coat came in, did a cursory exam, and said I had a minor upper arm sprain. I told her my wrist was really sore, my neck was hurting, and I had a terrific headache. She dismissed it entirely and sent me to physical therapy.

The Physical Therapist was more understanding and examined my wrist. She suspected that I had torn ligaments but could not treat me because the "doctor" had not written a prescription to treat my wrist, only my right upper arm. To this day I don't know how I survived the next four weeks. I saw the "doctor" once each week and the PT twice a week.

It was during my fourth follow-up visit to the "doctor" that I realized I had never been seen by a "doctor." That particular day the arrogant woman's white coat was buttoned up, and I could clearly read her name followed by the letters "PA" - I was horrified.

My apprehension was justified after I returned to my office at TBS that afternoon because a guardian angel in the Risk Management department called to tell me, "We're not satisfied with your lack of progress so we're sending you to a specialist."

It seems that under the care of the P.A. my shoulder had gotten much, much worse. Of course, I knew that, but the P.A. didn't listen. Within 24 hours I was on the exam table of a wonderful and well-qualified orthopedist who made a proper diagnosis the moment he walked in the door and saw me sitting on the table.

"You'll never use that arm again if you don't have surgery," he stated succinctly. "Of course, I'll verify my diagnosis with an MRI, but for the time being you're not to move that arm."

He later told me that he could diagnosis the injury because of the manner in which I was sitting and the unnatural hanging of my arm. He also said that any qualified physician would have immediately recognized the obvious symptoms of a torn rotator cuff.

I tried to show him the exercises the P.A. had prescribed, and he actually yelled at me, "Don't do that. Don't move that arm!"

Then he said in a calmer voice, "I'll never know how much more damage has been done because you should never have been allowed to move that arm with these injuries!!"

He was really mad. His assistant came in the room and put me in a shoulder restraint and they both gave me strict orders not to move my arm.

I was vindicated; the P.A. had made me feel like a hypochondriac and I actually had a serious shoulder injury. But that was not all she had misdiagnosed and mistreated. While in the hospital for shoulder surgery, Dr. Wonderful Orthopedist called in a neurosurgeon to examine my still hurting neck and head because my left arm had gone numb.

I left the hospital in a hard cervical collar with instructions not to move my head, lest I suffer permanent paralysis.

WHO'S WHO?

Before making your final selection, you might want to invest a little research time to answer these questions:

- Is your doctor/surgeon Board certified in their specialty?
- Are they a Fellow of the American College of Surgeons?
- How many of these surgeries has your doctor done?
- What is their success rate?
- What is the success rate of the hospital?
- How does that compare to national averages?

Selecting a medical team to guide your recovery is just the first step on the road to healing. If you have taken this first step you are ready to move on down the road to health. Hopefully, this book will give you the Guideposts you need to get you safely to your destination.

Chapter 2

Ready, Set, Go

When you are scheduled for surgery or long-term medical treatment, please don't overlook the mundane issues of life that can cause strife in relationships and undue stress while you are healing. If you have a spouse who already takes care of household matters, this won't apply. Lots of folks, however, need to think about these issues:

✓ **Your young children** – little folks can get emotionally stressed when separated from their parents, even if only a few days, so have a talk with them and explain it to them as simply and straight-forward as you can. Allow them to ask questions and answer them without drama or fear in your voice or demeanor. Children generally handle things better if they are informed and know what to expect.

You might want to make some of their favorite meals and put them in the freezer so they can enjoy your cooking while you are laid up.

If your children will be staying with family or friends while you are recuperating, pack their suitcases when you pack yours. Make it a fun experience for them and ask them what special toy or blanket or book they want to take.

Make a list of their daily habits, mealtimes, snacks, and bedtime rituals, and be sure to give their caretaker any medications or vitamins they need.

By all means, include the name of their pediatrician on your list, as well as your health insurance information. On a separate page write a letter "To Whom It May Concern" giving their caretaker the authority to have them treated for a medical emergency.

You might think this is a bit of over-planning, but such situations do arise. When I lived in Germany, I took care of many children who lived in our Army housing area. I always insisted on having this authorization letter – and I can't begin to tell you how many times I used it. None of them ever had an accident or injury while in my care, but flu, earaches, and upset stomachs were common. Your trip to the hospital does not preclude a medical situation for your children – so be prepared.

✓ **Your house** – who will look after your home in your absence, turn lights off and on, open and close windows, blinds or curtains, pick up messages on your answering machine, bring in the mail and newspapers, cut the lawn, water house plants, open and close the refrigerator on a regular basis, flush the toilets, turn the heat or air conditioning up and down, put out the garbage?

✓ **Your pets** – will you have a pet sitter coming by several times a day, will they be at the home of a friend or family member, or will they be boarded? Be sure you write out a daily schedule of the pet's usual activities and provide instructions for their food, medications, and any special routines such as walks, treats, and bedtimes. And you'll certainly want to leave the name and phone number of your Veterinarian in case of an emergency.

✓ **Your finances** – who will sort through your mail and take care of the bills? When my dear friend and next-door neighbor had back surgery that required a two-week hospital stay and four weeks in a rehabilitation center, she wrote out the checks for all her utilities, house note, church pledge, etc., before she left. She gave me the stack of checks with addressed envelopes and stamps.

When the mail came, I pulled out the bills, filled in the amount due (since the utility bills vary), and dropped them in the mail so everything was paid on time and she didn't have to bother with it at the hospital and in re-hab. Get someone you trust to do this.

Failure to plan the handling of your finances can cause major problems down the road, which could include aggravating effects such as late fees and utility turn-offs. You are supposed to be on road to wellness; you certainly don't want to take a detour because some financial boulders blocked your path. Let me give you just one little example of undue stress caused by finances.

> GUIDEPOST
>
> Prior planning before your surgery can save a lot of unnecessary stress.

A CASE STUDY:

Lost checks in the ICU

When I was a Red Cross volunteer at a large hospital in Atlanta, I was the liaison for the ICU – the go between person for the patients and their families.

We had a prominent gentleman who was admitted for surgery and he refused to turn over any responsibility for writing checks to his lovely, devoted wife. One evening, she showed up at visiting time with a large checkbook. She had to do payroll for more than twenty people, and he had to sign the checks. Well, as usual for an ICU unit, things were rather hectic, we had a code blue, and all the visitors were asked to leave. In her desperation to get their employees paid, she had him sign blank checks, pages and pages of them, and then she proceeded to lose the checkbook—and it was full of signed blank checks!!

We called security when we learned of her blunder and everyone available started looking for that checkbook. All the volunteers dropped what they were doing to join in the hunt, and we thoroughly searched the hospital.

She was lucky because we found it several hours later and all the checks were still in it. But it could have been a financial disaster. With a little planning, the entire stressful episode could have been prevented.

✓ **Your valuables** – you won't be worried about your fine jewelry if you take it to your safe deposit box before you go to the hospital.

If you have a security alarm in your house, you might consider giving the alarm system codes and password, along with a house key, to a neighbor you trust. There's nothing more aggravating than an alarm running for hours because no one knows how to disarm it.

If your neighborhood has a community watch program, be sure to tell them you'll be away so they can keep an eye on your house; better yet, tell your local police force if they have a surveillance program for absentee homeowners.

✓ **Your medications and nutritionals** – chances are, if you are having surgery, you have been prescribed medications and you might be on nutritional supplements, too. Make a complete list of everything you take, the times you take it, and pack them with your other items to go to the hospital. (More on this in Chapter 6….you'll save a lot of money if you provide your own.)

✓ **Your meals** – make a grocery list before your hospital stay so your caretaker will know what you like to eat. If you are particular about a brand, put that on your list, too.

If possible, buy your staples and supply your pantry ahead of time. Hopefully, however, you eat fresh fruits and vegetables. Since those have a short shelf-life, they should be purchased no more than a day before you come home.

While we are on the subject of short shelf-life, please clean out your refrigerator before you go to the hospital. In spite of all her good planning in other areas, my dear neighbor didn't think about the carton of milk, the pitcher of orange juice, the deli meats and cheeses, and the fruits and vegetables in her frig. Needless to say, it all became a stinky mess during her absence. She lost a lot of expensive food and the frig stunk for weeks after we cleaned it out.

If you're able, prepare some of your favorite meals and freeze one-meal portions in separate containers.

✓ **Your car** – vehicles take revenge when you don't pay attention to them. Their batteries die, their tires lose air, and they start to smell like dust bowls – or something worse.

Give your car keys to someone you trust and ask them to take the car for a spin around your neighborhood at least once a week. Put the windows down, and let it air out.

When you get back home, you'll want your car to be clean, so before you leave for *your repair job,* run your car through the wash, clean out any trash, and vacuum the floorboards.

✓ **Your family and friends** – gratitude and appreciation are important components of your healing (more on this in Section 3). Before your trip to the hospital, make a list of the people you know will either be with you or will visit, and then address a batch of envelopes for your "thank you" notes. Put a stamp on them and put a note card in each envelope, but don't seal it.

When someone comes to visit, or brings you something, you can pull out your pre-addressed envelopes, write a simple *thank you,* and show your gratitude and appreciation without the stress of looking for cards, addresses, and stamps.

I know most folks use electronic missives today, but there is nothing like a personal, hand-written note. Your friends and family will be pleased that you were so thoughtful and doing something for someone else will be good for you, too!

Now that you have made your lists and done some planning, it's time to get out your *Mending Map.*

Ready, set, go!

Chapter 3

Do No Harm

In the Hippocratic Oath doctors declare that they will "do no harm" in the treatment of their patients. We all know that many times it is the doctor who injures the patient, whether due to gross negligence or lack of skill or simply human error. The courts are overwhelmed with lawsuits against doctors, many of them unfounded, or simply someone trying to get rich off of their illness or injury by blaming innocent medical personnel. Some cases are so profound they make the national news, such as the case in Florida where a surgeon amputated the wrong leg.

What you don't hear about are the numbers of patients who have worsened their own condition and created more hardships simply because they did not know how to take care of themselves. It may be due to arrogance or ignorance, but the outcome is the same: They don't get better, they get worse.

It is easy to make errors in judgment when you are not feeling well, and those ill begotten ideas could end up doing you more harm than good. So, remember this: First, do no harm.

The Mending Map

If you are too ill to think things through, ask a family member or loved one to help you with this list:

- Do you understand the doctor's instructions? What were you told to do? Do you know how to do it?
- Did your doctor give you prescriptions for medications, physical therapy, or nutrition? Do you know why you were given these prescriptions?
- Does the druggist dispensing your medications understand the doctor's prescriptions?
- Do you understand the druggist instructions?
- Do you know which pills to take and when?
- Do you take them with food or without?
- Does your druggist know about *all* your meds, or just the new ones recently prescribed?
- Are you taking any supplements that could compromise the effectiveness of your prescription drugs? (See Appendix B for more information.)
- Are you afraid to mention these to your doctor or druggist? Why?
- Did the druggist tell you something different about your meds from what you understood the doctor to say?
- Does your Physical Therapist understand the doctor's prescription?
- Does your P.T. know about other conditions you may have that might affect your physical therapy?
- Do you understand the P.T.'s instructions?

- Did your P.T. give you written directions as well as pictures so you will know exactly what to do and how to do it?
- Did your P.T. give you advice about what you cannot do? Do you understand why you can't do that? (More about PT in Chapter 8.)
- Does your Nutritionist understand the doctor's prescriptions?
- Does the Nutritionist have information about food allergies you have?
- Does the Nutritionist know what drugs you are taking that might interact with certain foods?
- Did you understand the Nutritionist's menus? Can you carry out the instructions?
- Do you know what to eat and when? Do you know why this is important and what the benefits will be?
- Do you understand the consequences of not following instructions?
- If you don't understand the medical advice you are given, did you ask for clarification or simpler directions that you can follow?

Perhaps as you read this list you will think of other questions you can ask regarding medical care and following instructions.

A CASE STUDY:

First, do no harm

Several weeks after shoulder surgery, when I was on the road to recovery and no longer taking pain medications, I suddenly developed acute pain that was far worse than anything I had felt immediately after surgery. I suspected the cause was an extremely rough session with a Physical Therapist that left me in tears, but I understood my recovery would be painful and I did not complain. After two days of agony I called my surgeon's office and his assistant said he would phone in a prescription immediately for an anti-inflammatory drug. He said, "Follow the instructions on the label."

When I picked up the medicine at the drug store, the druggist said, "Take two with meals."

Anxious for relief, I quickly ate and took those pills with lunch. That evening, following the instructions on the label, "Take two with meals," I took two with dinner, and again the next day. The pills did not make me groggy; I was almost pain-free and working on a contract book and I didn't want pain to get in the way of my work. Other than some twinges of stomach discomfort I was feeling fairly good.

Three days later, with the original prescription for 20 pills reduced to four, and with much pain relief, I called my doctor's office to request a refill of the non-opioid drug.

"What," my doctor's assistant said. "You're almost out of that prescription? It was supposed to last for ten days!"

"Well, no," I explained. "I took it just as directed, two with meals. I took four the first day and six the next two days, so I only have four pills left. They are fantastic. No side effects and they don't make me drowsy at all."

"They wouldn't make you drowsy," he explained. "They are a new and powerful anti-inflammatory. I'm glad they worked but you should only take two a day, one in the morning with breakfast and one in the evening with dinner. That's all you should need. Any more than that can cause gastric distress."

"Oh," I said somewhat forlornly. "I've had two stomach ulcers and I have been having a little discomfort."

"Two a day," he reiterated. "I'll call the drug store right now. You can keep taking them, but only two a day."

I got the message. Only two a day. But the damage had been done. The old ulcer had been opened, and now I had to deal with stomach problems, too.

GUIDEPOST

Be sure you know exactly how to take the medicines you are prescribed.

A CASE STUDY:

Prescription drugs can kill you

My mother was a very gifted medical and scientific illustrator. She did drawings published in medical and dental textbooks, knew *Gray's Anatomy* (a standard medical school text for anatomy) backward and forward, and during her twenty-five-year career at the CDC in Atlanta, Mom worked on projects such as malaria, E-bola, salmonella, polio, small pox, and every parasitic organism that can invade the human body.

Mom was such an interesting person that whenever she went to the doctor, the conversation usually dwelt more on her work than her health challenge. She was generally healthy, stoic when ill, and never complained. However, a nagging attack of asthma that lasted for ten months finally prompted our family doctor to refer her to a specialist. Our family doctor had taken care of her for almost thirty years, and he knew that she could not tolerate certain drugs and was careful that they were never given to her.

The pulmonologist did not know Mom at all, but like other medical professionals he was fascinated with her work, which they apparently discussed in great detail while she was in his office. She left with three prescriptions, which she had filled at the pharmacy in the doctor's building.

Nine-years prior, Mom had had a valve in her heart replaced, and she always had her two maintenance drug prescriptions filled at her neighborhood pharmacy, where she and her druggist were on first-name basis. We have never understood why Mom had those three prescriptions from the pulmonologist filled at a different drug store. She called me the next afternoon to say that she had much relief from the asthma. That evening I cooked her 82nd birthday dinner and we had a grand time. She was lively and animated and breathing effortlessly. I was extremely relieved to see her feeling so well and never questioned what she was taking.

The next day, after church, while having Sunday dinner with five friends at a restaurant, she collapsed. Paramedics revived her at the restaurant, and she was transported to the closest hospital in very grave condition.

When I arrived, the doctor and nurses all told me, "We've never seen a case like this. She is hemorrhaging everywhere, her lungs, her kidneys, her brain."

They kindly cautioned me that I was in for a shock when I went in to see her. Blood was dripping out of her ears, nose, mouth, and the catheter bag was full of blood.

How could this happen? What had happened to this remarkable 82-year-old woman in good health, except for some asthma of unknown origin? Two hours later, only fifteen minutes before she passed on, my brother and his wife arrived from out of state. My sister-in-law, a chronic asthmatic, asked to see the drugs my mother was taking. We retrieved her purse, and Harriett withdrew three brown bottles, read the labels, and started to shake and cry.

"Your Mom should never have been on these drugs," she said through her tears. "She can't tolerate cortisone and two of these drugs have cortisone. It's no wonder she was feeling so much better so fast."

Yes, it's true. The drugs that cured Mom's asthma gave her the permanent cure. All that cortisone had caused a massive vascular collapse and she died.

My brother wanted to sue someone, but I challenged him, "Who are you going to sue? Obviously, the doctor who prescribed the drugs didn't know she can't take cortisone. I've never heard of this drug store, so they didn't have her medical records either. And the doctors and nurses here have certainly done everything humanly possible to save her."

Post-mortem investigations lead to the discovery of black mold in the air conditioning filters in Mom's apartment. That had caused the asthma. The coroner's office confirmed the emergency room doctor's diagnosis. Mother's heart was fine (she had no traces of atherosclerosis) and she had not had a stroke. The drugs had killed her.

My mother's case is not unusual. Please don't let it happen to you. If you are too embarrassed to discuss your prior medical history or problems with prescription drugs with your doctor, you've got the wrong doctor.

GUIDEPOST

Proper use of prescription drugs results in Adverse Drug Events (ADE) every year – accounting for 1 million emergency room visits and affecting 2 million hospital stays.

A CASE STUDY:

What in the world was he thinking?

One of my accounting clients is a contractor who builds high-end homes. Like many in his field he is a Type A personality, hardworking, self-motivated, and on the go constantly. He does not know the meaning of the phrase *slow down*. After a 30-foot fall backwards out of a third story window, he rolled, bounced up onto his feet, and hardly missed a beat. I mean, this man is tough.

But his back isn't. His lifestyle of off-road cycling, skiing, golf, and myriad other sporting activities plus the three-story fall all worked together to create an unbelievably severe back problem. A masterful neurosurgeon put his spine back together with an assortment of nuts and bolts, and within weeks the contractor returned to full-time work. He could not slow down. He ignored the advice not only of his surgeon but his fiancé and friends and family as well. The surgery was successful, but the patient was anything but patient.

When I met him, he was in acute pain again, barely two years after the surgery that had given him a new lease on life and all the strenuous activities he refused to give up. One weekend his right leg collapsed, and he fell flat on his face. After that, he could not pick up his foot; it would just flop. The surgeon operated again, this time removing the old hardware and putting in longer but lighter weight rods and pins. This spinal fusion was much longer than the previous one, running from T-12 (the last thoracic vertebrae) to L-5 (the fifth lumbar vertebrae). There was so much disease in one of the spinous process (the bone that juts out from the vertebrae) that it was three times normal size.

Two days later I was working in his basement office when he came home from the hospital. He bounced down the steps, declared he was 'doing great' and flopped into an easy chair to ice down his spine. In spite of the advice of everyone around him, he was on the job within a week, driving in two weeks, and the third weekend after four and a half hours of surgery, he went to a jobsite, loaded a bobcat onto a trailer all my himself, hooked up the trailer to a truck, and hauled the equipment to another site.

At this writing, he is writhing in pain. His back is severely swollen, his incision is oozing, and his arms are tingling. So, I asked him, "What in the world were you thinking?"

If you want to get well, first: DO NO HARM.

GUIDEPOST

If you want to get well, be your own best friend.

Chapter 4

Nutrition - You are what you eat

There are 75 trillion cells in your body. They make up the bones, muscles, cartilage, nerves, skin, hair, teeth, fingernails and toenails, veins and arteries, and a grand assortment of organs including the brain, intestinal tract, kidneys and urinary tract, eyes, and ears. When you are healthy you replace millions of cells every day. Skin cells are the fastest to be sloughed off and replaced, but you also replace cells that make up your internal organs, your bones, and your blood.

We all know that proper nutrition has a direct benefit to the body, and this is even more important when we are faced with the challenge of recovering from disease or injury. For example, if you break your leg, you can be sure you will need plenty of calcium rich foods and the attendant vitamins and minerals needed to build bone cells if you want your leg to heal properly.

If you have a brain, spinal cord, and neurological problem, your body will need plenty of good, vitamin B-complex foods. Eye problems need vitamin A rich foods, and foods with vitamin C helps skin to heal. (See Appendix A for *Foods that Heal*.)

Since you are constantly losing and rebuilding the cells in your body, you should give your body the nutrition it needs to build healthy replacement parts. There are also many illnesses that specifically restrict your diet. If you have diverticulitis, your doctor or dietitian has probably told you to avoid foods like nuts, which can exacerbate your condition. And if gout is your problem, you've probably been told to eliminate foods high in purines. (See more about purines in the notes about "Gout" in Appendix A.)

In my experience, few medical doctors are educated in nutrition, unless they are in a specialty that is related to the intestinal tract disorders, even though what you eat will have an impact on your health. (The exception, of course, would be physicians who treat diabetics and bariatric specialists who treat obesity.) What you eat directly affects your metabolism and your metabolism works in two ways: it either builds up new tissue (anabolism) or breaks down tissue (catabolism). If you are ill or injured, do you want to build new tissue or destroy what you already have?

The food you eat will either help you heal, or it will hinder your health. While you are laid up is an excellent time to read some books on nutrition and learn more about this vital part of your health. The last thing you need is more health problems because you put on weight while recuperating – which is what I did.

And please, don't get ambushed by "I don't feel good, I deserve a treat." I fell into this trap hook, line and sinker and I'm still paying the price.

> **GUIDEPOST**
>
> *Don't get hooked on bad food.*
> *Good nutrition is essential for getting better and staying healthy.*
>
> Foods that Harm, Foods that Heal
> Reader's Digest 1997, pg. 190

A CASE STUDY:

I deserve a treat

Before my fall at Turner Broadcasting, I was slim. I wore a size eight dress and looked great for my age, 54. Little did I know that I would be in re-hab for three years; nor did I appreciate the fact that decreased exercise (up till then I walked two to three miles a day and exercised regularly) and dietary changes would put me into the over-weight bordering on obese category.

Looking back on it I realize I did everything wrong. I had physical therapy three to five times a week. After shoulder surgery, the sessions were particularly brutal, and I always soothed my raw nerves with a trip to the Starbucks across the street from the hospital. A large coffee and yummy pastry were just what I needed. I had been through an ordeal and I would tell myself *I deserve a treat*.   **no, no, no**

Although I ate low-fat muffins, I was still consuming calories. And it is calories, my friend, that make you fat. In the next three years, I put on twenty pounds! That's right, twenty pounds. And after knee and foot surgery, I gained another ten. I went from being a slender, agile middle-age woman to an over-weight dowdy old lady. My self-esteem plummeted just when I needed it the most. I no longer saw myself as an energetic contributor to society who enjoyed life to the fullest. I was fat and ugly, and never felt good.

And I had no one to blame but myself. Had I realized what I was doing, I would have done things differently. I could still have a treat, but I would limit it to a small black coffee and handful of nuts from my own kitchen. The nuts would give me some much-needed protein, and their fatty acids would give me a natural anti-inflammatory (more on this in the supplements chapter). The protein would help curb my appetite while giving me the nutrition I needed for cell repair. So, when it comes to treats, please don't do what I did.

GUIDEPOST

The greatest gift you can give yourself is a return to good health.

Nutrition for Convalescents

Believe it or not, you can develop malnutrition in the hospital. I know a clinical pharmacist who practiced at a large, well-respected hospital in Atlanta and he told me about a patient who died of a brain disorder as a result of insufficient copper. The man was admitted for surgery and had some complications; however, his brain was fine when admitted.

He was put on intravenous fluids and tube feeding but apparently no one thought to take a look at his nutritional needs. Due to his condition, his absorption of copper was extremely low and because his hospital intake contained no copper, his brain was damaged beyond repair and he died.

Although this may seem to be an extreme example, it does happen. When patients receive only intravenous fluids for long periods of time, malnutrition can develop. If you or a loved-one is in the hospital for more than a few days, be sure to talk to the hospital dietitian about the essential nutrients – vitamins and minerals. No one lives and no one recovers without them. No one!

I take a lot of supplements and every time I go to the hospital I have them with me; I've never been told "No," that I can't have them. As mentioned earlier, you do need to know if specific nutritional supplements may interfere with certain medications or surgical procedures. (See Appendix B for *Herb, Drug, and Supplement Interactions*.)

There are thousands of books on nutrition, so I am listing just a few of the situations where nutrition makes a big impact. (See Appendix A for *Foods can Harm, Foods can Heal*).

Nutrition for your Immune System

If you are sick or injured, your immune system is in overdrive, and is most likely fighting a war on two fronts: the external assault from bacteria and/or viruses and the internal assault of free radicals and disease. The weapons your immune system needs are Proteins, Fatty Acids, and the Vitamins and Minerals that make up the Antioxidant Family. Let's take a look at each:

Proteins

Think of antibodies as the bullets in your immunity defense system. Antibodies are made by amino acids and amino acids come from proteins.

> Proteins ⟶ Amino acids ⟶ Antibodies

Your body only metabolizes (creates) some of the twenty amino acids you need; the remaining nine must come from your food. For that reason, they are called "essential" amino acids – if you don't eat them, you don't have them.

When you realize that about three-fourths of the solid part of your body is protein, you can understand the need for adequate protein intake – especially when you are healing. Proteins also build cells, enzymes, and hormones.

You can't store protein, which is needed in large amounts when new tissues are being built, so you need a good daily supply. However, please don't think you need to eat a big steak every day in order to heal. There are plenty of plant sources of amino acids.

Sources of protein include poultry, fish, lean meats, egg whites, legumes – soy and soy products such as tofu – beans and peas, nuts and seeds, certain whole grain breads and pasta, and brown rice.

In some cases, you may need to supplement with amino acids, but don't make this decision on your own. You should only take amino acid supplements under the guidance to a health practitioner who knows how to diagnose your specific nutritional requirements and make sound recommendations.

Fatty Acids

Even though fat gets blasted in the media, it is not the nutritional outlaw it has been made out to be. Your body will not function without it and when you consider that mother's milk is almost 50% fatty acids, you can begin to appreciate its importance. In fact, cholesterol is so important to your body that your liver makes what you need, and you won't have healthy cell membranes and nerves without it.

Did you know that your brain is almost 60% fat? Emerging research suggests that one of the reasons for the rise in Alzheimer's in the last decade is the long-term use of statin drugs, which lower cholesterol.

For a healthy immune system, you need a daily supply of good fatty acids for energy and to transport vitamins A, D, E and K into the cells where they can work to help you heal. Some of the omega-3s and the omega-6 fatty acids will help you fight infection, reduce inflammation, and are helpful in the fight against heart disease. Fatty acids are also essential for proper brain function. Unfortunately, your body does not make these two fatty acids; therefore, it is essential that you have them in your diet.

> GUIDEPOST
>
> *...over 50 different conditions of the brain may be associated with fatty acid imbalance or insufficiency.*
>
> -Dr Michael Schmidt, co-author
> *Bio-Age: 10 Steps to a Younger You* (King 2002)

Sources of good fatty acids are fish (herring, tuna, mackerel, and sardines), flax seeds, and walnuts. I personally take 1,000 mg. of organic flax seed oil with every meal because my dad had severe arthritis and I've had a number of broken bones and soft tissue injuries. I'm 75 years old and have no arthritis.

Antioxidants

If vitamins and minerals were people with jobs in our society, the antioxidants would be the guys who work for the sheriff: They round up all the bad guys — the free radicals — and send them off to jail where they can't hurt anyone. I like to call them the Aces – Vitamins A, C, E and the mineral Selenium.

Free radicals can't help it that they cause so much damage. They are just a natural by-product of the millions of chemical reactions that take place in our bodies. For that reason, they need to be held in custody and then neutralized by a healthy immune system.

ACE

Each of the ACEs has a specific job and together they get a lot done. Vitamin A helps ward off infection, Vitamin C helps build new tissue and also fight infection, Vitamin E helps cells repair and rejuvenate, and Selenium aids in antibody production and helps keep your liver and heart healthy.

Sources of Vitamins A and C include leafy vegetables and fruits; Vitamin E is in wheat germ and nuts, and

Selenium is in Brazil nuts, cashews, other tree nuts, and almonds (humm…seems those almonds keep popping up).

Nutrition for Constipation

One of the unpleasant side effects of being confined to bed during recuperation is constipation, which can be due to a number of factors. But you don't need to suffer if you know why you may have this condition and what to do about it.

Antibiotics, one of the miracle drugs of the 20th century, are often prescribed to post-surgical patients to either prevent or treat a bacterial infection. But a side effect, constipation, can be caused when the necessary and naturally occurring good bacteria in your intestines are killed off by these medicines. Although bacteria usually get bad press, the fact is you could not live without the good guys in your gut. A properly functioning intestinal tract will have millions and millions of friendly bacteria that break down food so its nutrients can be assimilated through the wall of the gut into the blood stream. This process also contributes to good bowel function because the leftover particles are small enough to pass through the intestinal track.

When the good guys are not there to do their job, not only do you not have good bowel motility, more than likely you don't have good absorption either. This is a double whammy because you need those nutrients that are now stuck in your gut. You are already uncomfortable from your illness or injury, and now you are constipated, which adds to your distress.

For whatever reason, most physicians overlook this situation and only prescribe laxatives or stool softeners for antibiotic or immobility related constipation. Of course, this does not cure the condition; it only treats the side effect of the antibiotic. A more realistic treatment would be to cure the problem and that can only be done by adding back into your system the good bacteria it needs.

Nutritionists who specialize in this area of health will tell you that you need to "re-flora" by taking a supplement you can purchase at the health food store. There are numerous brands with various mixes of these good bacteria that will restore motility and proper assimilation of the nutrients your body needs to get well. It's important to remember that these good guys *should not* be taken within FOUR hours of the antibiotic. Otherwise, they too will be killed off.

Another source of good bacteria is yogurt so you might want to give this a try if your medical condition does not limit your intake of dairy products. Whatever course you take, do something to correct constipation so your intestinal track will be able to properly absorb the nutrients you need and also eliminate the waste you don't need.

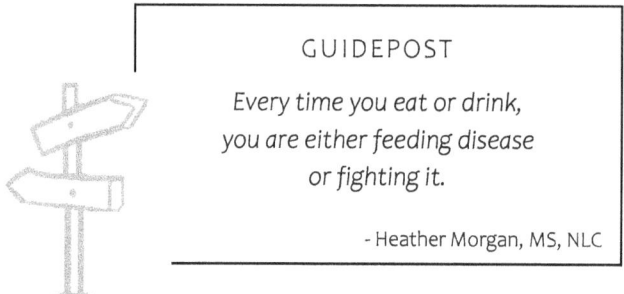

GUIDEPOST

*Every time you eat or drink,
you are either feeding disease
or fighting it.*

- Heather Morgan, MS, NLC

Herbs can also be helpful for your digestive health and here a few that you may want to try:

LAVENDER – since your digestion can be slowed by tension and anxiety about your condition, lavender can help keep things moving along by calming the intestines.

OREGANO – this herb is very alkaline, so it helps fight inflammation and acidity.[7]

PEPPERMINT – for constipation, diarrhea, bloating, gas and indigestion, fresh peppermint is a good choice. It's also useful in tea form.[8]

ROSEMARY – this is another good herb for indigestion, gas, constipation, and bloating.

SAGE – this herb will help you dispel gas and also help your stomach digest protein.

THYME – have a tummy virus? The antiviral compounds in thyme can help.

BE a NUT about your Health! "People who eat nuts are less likely to die from heart disease, respiratory disease or cancer than people who do not eat nuts." [9]

GUIDEPOST

Our food should be our medicine and our medicine should be our food.

-Hippocrates

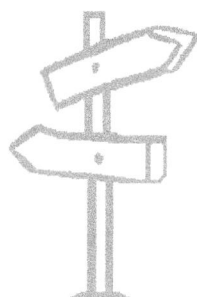

GUIDEPOST

You are what you eat.
If you want to BE well,
EAT well.

Chapter 5

It's sleepy time

Sleep is an essential component of good health and vital when we are recovering from illness or injury, but unfortunately many of us can't sleep well when we are sick or in pain. Chronic pain can cause a depletion of serotonin, which in turn leads to sleep disorders since serotonin is necessary for sleep.

Lack of sleep exacerbates pain and we get caught up in a cycle of poor sleep and chronic pain. This slows our recovery as stage 3 restorative sleep is essential to healing.

In addition, when we don't get enough sleep, we tend to eat foods that are higher in calories and carbohydrates. So, let's review some basic information about sleep so all this will make sense. There are four stages of sleep:

Stage 1: The transition period from being awake to deep sleep; your brain waves start to slow down from your active awake state.

Stage 2: The intermediate phase; 40% to 50% of total sleep time is in stage 2. During this phase your body temperature drops, muscles relax, breathing and heartbeat slow, and eye movement stops.

Stage 3: This is the most restorative phase of sleep and consists of slow delta waves. During this non-REM sleep (REM – Rapid Eye Movement) your breathing, heartbeat, and brainwaves are their slowest and your muscles are most relaxed. For these reasons, it's harder to awaken from this deep sleep stage than the others.

Stage 4: About 90 minutes after falling asleep, eye movement increases (REM) along with heartbeat, breathing, and brain wave activity but arm and leg muscles are "paralyzed" to prevent you from hurting yourself from acting out your dreams, which occur during this stage. Although you can dream during any sleep stage, most dreams occur in the REM phase.

To improve your chances of a good, restorative sleep, here are some things to keep in mind:

- Have a regular bedtime and use your bedroom for sleep only – not as an office or home gym. This way your body will associate your bedroom with sleep.
- Don't eat spicy foods, or drink alcohol or caffeine at least four to six hours before bedtime.
- Don't exercise or do your physical therapy within two hours of bedtime (unless, for some reason, your medical professional prescribes PT before bed).

- Take a warm bath, read a good book (nothing violent), listen to relaxing music.
- Turn off overhead and bright lights, electronics, cell phones, and television.
- If you need it, have a bed-time drink with one of these sleep inducing beverages:

   Honey: This sweet treat is a tranquilizer and sedative, so a tablespoon in some herbal tea can help you get some zzzz's.

   Malted Milk: Although mostly used for flavoring in the USA, malted milk is easy to digest and can be good for convalescents; because it also induces sleep, it can be a good choice in lieu of habit-forming sleeping pills. Milk has a lot of tryptophan, an amino acid, making a natural "sleep aid" because it boosts serotonin, the brain chemical that induces sleep.

   Warm Milk: The amino acid L-tryptophan in milk is converted to 5-HTP and releases serotonin, which is relaxing. It's also high in calcium, which promotes sleep.[10]

Because certain foods contain the amino acid, tryptophan, and tryptophan is a precursor for melatonin[11] - the sleep hormone - you are naturally going to feel drowsy after eating those foods. In addition to our diets, sleep can also be affected by certain medications – so ask your pharmacist about your prescription drugs and how they can affect your sleep. Here is a list of some of the foods you should consider eating - or not eating - when you are preparing for bedtime:

To sleep well:

DO EAT THESE	BECAUSE
Almonds	Tryptophan, magnesium – steady the heart but slow muscle and nerve function
Oatmeal, Whole grain bread	Glucose spike is followed by lower energy
Honey	Glucose tells brain to turn off orexin, the "alert" chemical
Cherries	Natural source of melatonin, the sleep hormone
Dark chocolate	Serotonin, relaxes body and mind
Hummus	Tryptophan, helps induce sleep
Bananas	Magnesium and potassium – muscles and nerves relax; B_6 converts to tryptophan and serotonin
DON'T EAT THESE	**BECAUSE**
Aged Cheese, Soy, Processed meats	Amino acid tyramine is a stimulant
Spicy foods, Tomato sauces	Heartburn, acid reflux
Alcohol	Won't enter a deep sleep stage
Milk chocolate	Contains dopamine, a stimulant
Ginseng tea	Stimulant

Sleep is vital to your health and your recovery, so you should seek medical intervention if your insomnia is persistent. Your medical professional can evaluate other causes such as sleep apnea or a circadian rhythm problem.

Plenty of good sleepy time is essential to your recovery, so please don't ignore or minimize this guidepost on your mending map.

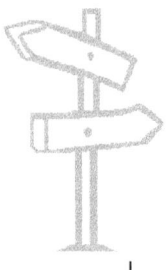

GUIDEPOST

[Acupuncture] reduces pain and anxiety, stabilizes blood-sugar and cholesterol levels, and improves sleep and body functioning—all of which help the body fight back.

- Dr. Semmler de la Torre

GUIDEPOST

Your body recovers at night during sleep.

Chapter 6

Herbs and Supplements

Please don't pooh-pah the idea of herbs and supplements! Very few people get the nutrients they need from food, especially if they are recovering from illness or injury. Different ailments require different nutrients. Find out from your doctor or nutritionist exactly what you need and buy them from a reputable health food store (most of the national brands are poor quality).

Herbs can also be remarkably effective, but you need to be sure there will not be any negative reactions with your prescription drugs. Ask your doctor or pharmacist. If the label does not say "Standardized" you're wasting your money.

When we refer to "supplements" we are talking about vitamins, minerals, and enzymes. These *micro-nutrients* are essential for your health but you only need them in miniscule amounts. Foods (carbohydrates, proteins, and fat) are *macro-nutrients* because they are needed in larger quantities. Let's take a look at these micro-nutrients first:

ENZYMES

Enzymes are required for everything your body does—seeing, thinking, smelling, breathing, tasting, talking, playing and walking, to name just a few. You can't have life without enzymes because they are in every living thing. Most of your enzymes are manufactured in your body by proteins. There are two types of enzymes in your body: metabolic and digestive.

>**Metabolic enzymes** run the body and make repairs.

>**Digestive enzymes** help you process carbohydrates and fat and turn them into fuel your body can use.

A third type of enzyme is found in raw foods. They start food digestion and help the body's own digestive enzymes so they don't have to work so hard.

<u>**Co-Enzyme Q-10**</u> - You've probably heard Co-enzyme Q-10 mentioned in news and ads the last few years, but those of us in the wellness arena have been touting its benefits since the 1990s. This organic compound, which is actually an antioxidant, is found in every cell of the human body and is so important that Dr. Peter Mitchell, an English bio-chemist, was awarded the Nobel Prize in 1978 for his work to identify the role of Co-Q-10 in the human body.

>As we age, our bodies generate less Co-Q-10, which is why supplementation can be extremely beneficial, especially to heart patients. If you have low energy, you may also have low Co-Q-10.

>Certain medications, such as the statins that are prescribed for high cholesterol, rob the body of Co-Q-10. We

can only wonder how much damage is done as a result of this assault on an essential component of the cells.

Pharmaceutical companies have finally come around to admitting that there is a problem with statins, and that they do compromise Co-Q-10; they now recommend taking a supplement to offset this undesirable side effect.

If you are taking a statin, be sure that you take your Co-Q-10 at the opposite time of day; otherwise, you will receive no benefit because the chemicals in statin drugs that kill your enzymes that create cholesterol also kill off your Co-Q-10. Talk to your doctor or nutritionist about this.

Enzymes, which are really sophisticated proteins, don't work by themselves. They need help from vitamins or minerals to get their jobs done. If your health is challenged, you should talk to your medical professional or nutritionist to see if enzyme supplements are suitable for your particular situation.

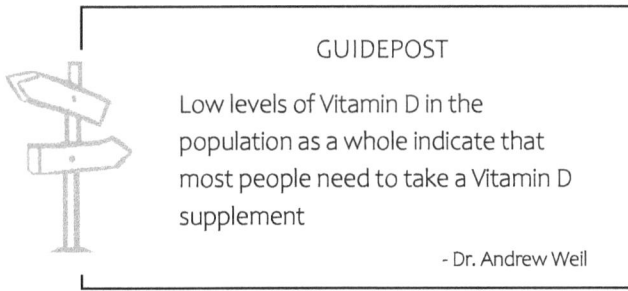

GUIDEPOST

Low levels of Vitamin D in the population as a whole indicate that most people need to take a Vitamin D supplement

- Dr. Andrew Weil

VITAMINS

Vitamins are helper micro-nutrients for converting food into energy and manufacturing blood cells. As chief assistants to enzymes they help activate the never ending chain of chemical reactions in our bodies. Healthy cells cannot be maintained without vitamins.

There are two types of vitamins: fat soluble and water soluble. Fat soluble vitamins (A, D, E, and K) can be stored in body fat and used later. If too many of these are accumulated in body tissues they may create toxic effects.

The water soluble vitamins are the eight Bs and C. Because they dissolve in body fluids, excesses are eliminated by urine or sweat.

In 1943, the U.S. Government recommended that certain amounts of vitamins be included in food served to the Armed Forces. These RDAs (Recommended Dietary Allowances) are updated every five years and indicate only the average amounts needed by healthy people to prevent deficiency diseases. For optimum health, many nutritional experts recommend quantities much higher than the RDAs.

If you have a chronic disease, infection, or cancer, if you smoke, drink alcohol, take certain vitamin depleting medications, or have excessive stress (either emotional or environmental) in your life, you could require a lot more vitamins than the RDA.

Elderly people, dieters, pregnant or lactating women, and people recovering from surgery should consider supplementing their diets with extra vitamins but no one should ever mega-dose on vitamins without proper oversight by a medical professional or nutritionist.

After I had meningitis, my neurologist mega-dozed me for almost a year on some of the B-vitamins, and due to other challenges to my central nervous system, years later I still need more B-complex than most people. Everyone has their own needs, so don't compromise your health by taking a dosage that might not be optimum for you. Here are some basics on vitamins:

Vitamin A - builds immune response, keeps mucous membranes moist; important for growth and healthy skin; deficiency causes night blindness. It is toxic in large doses. Found in beta-carotene, a component of carrots, as well as broccoli and spinach.

Vitamin B-1 - Thiamine - is beneficial to nervous system; promotes growth in children, strengthens immune system, assists in metabolizing carbohydrates. Deficiency causes fatigue, insomnia. Found in asparagus, brown rice, brewer's yeast, beans, whole grains, nuts and seeds, and wheat germ.

Vitamin B-2 - Riboflavin - necessary for energy production, this vitamin is frequently lacking in American diets. Necessary for the eyes and healthy skin. Found in almonds, brewer's yeast, broccoli, leafy green vegetables, yogurt, wild rice, and mushrooms.

Vitamin B-3 - Niacin - is required by many body systems including digestion, production of energy, metabolizing cholesterol, sex hormone synthesis, skin and nerves. Deficiency leads to skin problems, headaches, possible high blood pressure, and mental problems. Found in almonds, avocados, bananas, brewer's yeast, legumes, and whole grains.

Vitamin B-5 - Pantothenic Acid - is needed by adrenal glands for cortisone production to prevent arthritis and high cholesterol. Builds antibodies, fights stress and nerve disorders. Deficiency causes anemia. Found in brown rice, brewer's yeast, broccoli, legumes, yams, and whole grains.

Vitamin B-6 - Pyridoxine - essential for red blood cells, amino acids and metabolism, healthy skin and nerves. Important immune stimulant. Deficiency causes depression, anemia, and skin lesions. Found in avocados, bananas, brewer's yeast, buckwheat, legumes, and nuts.

Vitamin B-12 - Cyano Cobalamin - vital for proper functioning of central nervous system and red blood cell formation. Deficiency can cause paralysis and death, but symptoms of depletion may not appear for five years since it is stored in the body. B-12 is synthesized in the body but is also found in yeast grown on a B-12 medium, spirulina and soy sauce.

Biotin - is a member of the B-complex vitamin family. It is needed for amino acid and essential fatty acid metabolism. Deficiency results in skin and muscle problems. Found in brewer's yeast, grapefruit, raspberries, and tomatoes

Choline - is another member of the B-complex family; necessary for proper brain and neurotransmitter functioning as it is the precursor to acetylcholine. It can be effective in treatment for Alzheimer's and nervous system disorders. Found in unrefined vegetable oils, legumes, and soy products.

Folic Acid - a B-Complex component, is required for production of DNA, blood, enzyme efficiency, and vital for new cells. Deficiency creates digestive system problems. Found in brewer's yeast, broccoli, soy products, and leafy green vegetables.

Inositol - another member of the B-complex family but not a vitamin. It works with biotin and choline; lowers cholesterol and controls fatty deposits. Aids in control of diabetic complications. Found in almonds, beans, oranges, onions, peanut butter, oats, peas, tomatoes, and zucchini.

PABA - Para-Aminobenzoic Acid - also a B-complex family member and component of folic acid. Is effective as a sun screen and treatment of burns and vitiligo. Found in brewer's yeast, molasses and wheat germ.

Vitamin C - Ascorbic Acid - is essential for the immune system and forming new collagen. Works as an anti-oxidant to fight free radicals. Speeds healing, effective in treating colds and other viruses, and lowering cholesterol. Found in citrus fruits, green peppers, papaya, tomatoes, potatoes, greens, kiwi, cauliflower and broccoli.

Bioflavonoids - are part of the C complex and help it function. They are also effective in preventing hardening of the arteries and enhance strength of the circulatory system (blood vessels, veins, and capillaries). Bioflavonoids protect connective tissues, help lower cholesterol, and stimulate bile production. Because your body does not manufacture its own supply of this nutrient, it is important to get it in supplements and food sources such as buckwheat, most vegetables, and the white inside of citrus fruit skins.

Vitamin D - can be synthesized by the body from sunlight. Working with Vitamin A it utilizes phosphorus and calcium to build bones and teeth. Effective in treating eye problems and protects against colon cancer. Found in cod liver oil.

Emerging research indicates that Vitamin D-3 receptors can be found on every cell in the body, and deficiency in this vital nutrient may be one of the causes of breast cancer. In 2006 the CDC reported that a whopping one-fourth of the population was deficient in vitamin D.[12]

Vitamin E - Tocopherol - stimulates the immune system and retards cellular aging. Improves skin and works with selenium to fight free radicals. Deficiency results in nerve and muscle degeneration and anemia. Found in almonds, leafy vegetables, soy products, wheat germ, beans and peas.

Vitamin K - is essential for blood clotting. Helps heal broken blood vessels in the eye and prevents bone loss. Metabolized normally in the intestinal track, it can be eaten in leafy green vegetables, potatoes, bran, yogurt, and tomatoes. Vitamin K also works with calcium to make bone cells.

RNA - Ribonucleic Acid - a natural substance that is thought to be an important ingredient in the brain's chemistry and is nicknamed the "memory molecule." It also helps improve skin tone and appearance. Found in yeast.

GUIDEPOST

You take the healthiest diet in the world, if you gave those people vitamins, they would be twice as healthy. So vitamins are valuable.

-Dr. Robert Atkins

MINERALS

Like vitamins, minerals are needed to jump start the enzymes—they just don't get going without mineral aid. Minerals unite nutrients with your cells, the way mortar holds the bricks on your house together. They also keep the body pH in balance, making sure that it is alkaline and not acid. Minerals transport oxygen, regulate the beating of your heart, help form bones, digest food, keep your furnace (metabolism) running, and assist in balancing you mentally and emotionally.

There are two groups of minerals. The <u>essential minerals</u> are calcium, magnesium, and phosphorus. The <u>trace minerals</u> are copper, chromium, iron, iodine, manganese, potassium, selenium, and zinc. Minerals are all over the body, but their main home is bone and muscle tissue.

Essential Minerals:

<u>Calcium</u> is necessary for strong bones and teeth, and is especially important in growing children, pregnant women, and elderly people. It is the most abundant mineral in your body—you have about two and a half pounds (1,200 grams). The Framingham Heart Study discovered that men who ate higher levels of calcium had a lower risk for developing hypertension.[13] Source? Leafy vegetables.

<u>Magnesium</u> works with calcium for teeth and bone formation. It is also important for muscles and nerve function. My druggist put me on magnesium oxide for a lung problem since I don't trust asthma drugs; my pulmonologist says I have a remarkably high level of function, even with a significant lung impairment, and to keep taking what the

druggist suggested. Source? Peanuts, beans, and whole grains.

Phosphorus is the third essential for bones and teeth. It is also needed to get oxygen to the brain, for proper cell growth and nervous system function. About one percent of your weight is phosphorus. Source? It is found in many, many foods and we usually have enough in our diets.

Trace Minerals:

Copper helps in your iron absorption, protein metabolism, bone mineralization, blood clotting and formation. Source? Raisins, sea vegetation such as kelp, high fiber cereals, nuts, and legumes.

Chromium is essential, even in trace amounts, for proper glucose regulation. Nutritionists recommend 200 to 600 mcg daily, but the average American only gets about 25 mcg in their diet, so many people are supplementing their diets with chromium picolinate or chromium polynicotinate acid. Exercise increases the need for chromium supplementation. Source? Brewer's yeast, honey, whole grains, grapes, and raisins.

Iron joins proteins and copper to make hemoglobin, the messengers that carry oxygen to your cells. Without sufficient iron the tissues become starved for oxygen and you feel tired. But too much iron can be very toxic, especially in children, who can be innocently killed by iron overdoses when they eat iron supplements[14] intended for adults. Source? Leafy green vegetables, prunes, legumes, and whole grains.

Iodine is necessary for proper thyroid function and metabolism, healthy hair, skin, and nails. Source? Sea vegetables.

Manganese nourishes the brain and nerves. It also helps metabolize fats and sugar. Manganese supplements should be taken under the guidance of a health professional as high levels can cause a person to become violent. Source? Bananas, pineapple, green vegetables, whole grains, nuts, and cereals.

Potassium is very popular with your cells - they have more of this mineral than any other. It is needed for proper nerve function and helps maintain the amount of fluid in your cells. Heart patients or people taking diuretics may need potassium supplements, but increasing consumption should only be done under guidance of a health professional. Because it must be in balance with sodium, too much sodium from processed foods can increase the need for potassium. There is no RDA for this mineral. Source? Fresh foods and legumes.

Selenium works with vitamins A and C to produce an antioxidant effect and fight free radicals. Source? Sea kelp, garlic, brewer's yeast, wheat germ, and sesame seeds.

Zinc is vital for proper immune system performance and development of insulin. Because of its effect on the brain, it can be effective in the treatment of nerve related disorders. Two symptoms of zinc deficiency are loss of taste and smell.

Since those are also two of the symptoms of the COVID-19 virus, I ask myself how many people are suffering from this terrible virus who might possibly be helped by inexpensive supplementation with zinc? Zinc is also important for healthy hair and skin. Do not take zinc supplements for long periods of time because it must be in balance with copper. If zinc is needed, a health professional should monitor your supplementation program. Source? Mushrooms, brewer's yeast, and wheat germ.

You must eat foods that contain minerals since your cells cannot manufacture (synthesize) them. Because minerals make up four percent of your body weight, you can see how important they are.

Herbs, vitamins, and minerals can be wonderful companions on your trip along the mending map, and indeed, they are essential components for your healing.

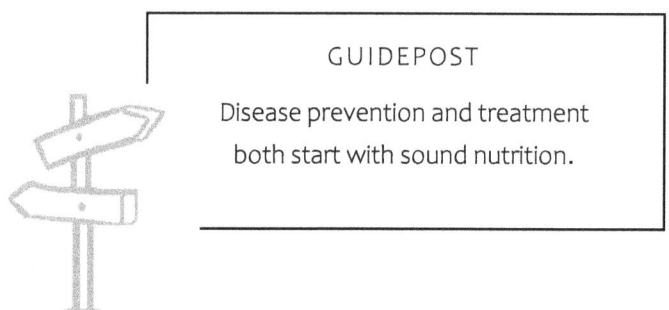

GUIDEPOST

Disease prevention and treatment both start with sound nutrition.

Chapter 7

Don't Fear Alternatives

Do yourself a favor and be open-minded. No one person has all the answers and sometimes it's better to have a team. Yes, of course you have faith in the primary *Guide* we talked about in Chapter 1 – BUT, what if you can't find one?

You may have a complex situation that is difficult to diagnose and treat, or perhaps you have been misdiagnosed. Maybe there is no one in your geographic area who is an expert in your health challenge and you don't want to travel.

The key to the state of wellness will belong to the person who knows that there are many modalities available today and is willing to give complementary, integrative or alternative therapies an opportunity to work for them.

If you are sick and tired of being sick and tired maybe it's time to learn about some of the many paths you can take to wellness. So, what are these alternative modalities and therapies that can lead you to wellness? We'll list the various practices first and then we'll discuss some of the alternative therapies.

Acupuncture has been used for thousands of years. It is an ancient Chinese method of healing that uses needles to realign the energy that flows through the body. By inserting exceptionally fine needles at various meridian points, the energy that flows to specific organs can be manipulated. Acupuncture is widely accepted throughout the United States and is effective in the treatment of chronic pain and is known to increase endorphins and serotonin.[15]

Chiropractors treat misalignment of nerve pathways that cause disease and pain. By manipulation of the spine, or other areas of the body, stress that caused the illness or pain is relieved. It is particularly useful in the treatment of back and joint pain associated with muscle spasms. Most chiropractors are also well educated in nutritional therapies that can treat other medical problems.

Holistic doctors look at the whole person to diagnose and treat disease rather than depending upon one system or part. They believe that the mind, body, and spirit must all be employed if the patient is to become well. Many holistic practitioners use a variety of modalities that may include acupuncture, chiropractic, homeopathy, aromatherapy, allopathy, iridology, herbal therapies, and vitamin/mineral supplementation.

Homeopathy treats *like with like*. For instance, a person with insomnia might be treated with a minuscule portion of caffeine that alters the flow of the life force in the body, resulting in a peaceful sleep. It is especially effective in the treatment of chronic problems such as allergies, arthritis and hypertension.

Because homeopathy relies heavily on the body to heal itself over a period of time, it should never be used in the case of medical emergency or serious infection. Homeopathy, as it is practiced today, has been used more than 200 years, although the basis for this ancient healing art has been known for thousands of years. Writing in *Health Counselor* newsletter Frances FitzGerald says that "...there is an increasing dissatisfaction over mainstream medicine's expense, questionable effectiveness, and sometimes dangerous side effects."[16] She goes on to say that "many physicians and patients agree that homeopathy, a natural healing science, deserves a closer look."[17]

     This field of medical science holds much promise for non-invasive treatment of numerous medical maladies in the future. And homeopathy is now being used by holistic veterinarians with astounding success.[18] Here in the year 2020, there is continued dissatisfaction in health care, yet homeopathy is still not a mainstream modality. Why?

Iridologists diagnose disease and imminent illness by studying the iris of the eye. Meridian points of the body are reflected in the iris and study of the texture and structure of the iris can lead to non-invasive diagnosis. Iridology is a diagnostic tool used by many health practitioners, including medical doctors.

Kinesiology employs the neuro-muscular system for diagnosis and treatment. It is sometimes called A.K., or applied kinesiology.

Naturopaths use natural therapies that enable the body to heal without invasive procedures. They believe that disease is caused by lack of proper maintenance of the body allowing the immune system to be overtaken by poor lifestyle factors such as stress and improper nutrition.

Osteopathy is based on the theory that a sound body depends upon the health and maintenance of the body's structures. Although osteopaths may use their hands-on approach to diagnose disease and manipulate body structures to treat problems, many today conduct their practices along the lines of allopathic medical doctors by prescribing drugs and using x-rays. There are also osteopathic specialists and surgeons such as urologists and orthopedists and my gynecologist, who is a DO and one of the leading cancer specialists in this area.

With all these choices, how do you choose a reliable health practitioner?

First:
- Get references from friends or family members; advertisements can be misleading or even false.
- Ask your reference how they were helped.
- Was the therapy beneficial?
- Was it reasonably priced?
- Was the office staff competent and professional?

Second:
- Check out the doctor's credentials.
- What do all those initials after their name mean?
- Where did they receive their formal education?
- What health associations have admitted them as members?

Third:
- Watch for exorbitant claims. Do they claim to have secret knowledge or a cure-all pill?
- If so, you'll want to avoid them.

Now let's take a look at some of the many complementary, alternative, or integrative therapies that are available:

Aromatherapy uses fragrances from plants, flowers, and fruits for relaxation and pain relief from disorders such as headaches, arthritis, and nasal congestion. Various aromatic oils are used to treat certain maladies but should not be taken internally. Use them only by inhalation under the supervision of a licensed practitioner or by rubbing diluted oils into the skin.

Biofeedback monitors skin temperature, muscle tension, and other bodily processes by using sensors that send data to a machine. The machine continually produces a graph of the patient's responses and by watching the readings patients learn to control their thoughts and movements. Biofeedback is effective in pain control as well as other disorders such as hypertension, psychological phobias, and anxiety.

EFT Emotional Freedom Technique is a relatively new modality for treating emotional, mental and physical ailments with a painless procedure of tapping on various meridian points in the body. (See more about EFT in Chapter 16). A simplified way to think of Energy Psychology procedures is to view them as acupuncture for the emotions, but without the needles. These methods have already been applauded by self-help gurus Wayne Dyer and Tony Robbins, self-esteem expert Nathaniel Brandon, renowned physicists like William Tiller, and best-selling microbiologist Candace Pert.

Fasting helps your cells eliminate toxic accumulations. During a fast the body burns damaged or diseased parts which are then expelled through the skin, lungs, kidneys or colon. There are many types of cleansing and detoxifying fasts, which can last from one to ten days. Many people who fast regularly report they are not only physically healthier, but also enjoy a heightened awareness and more positive outlook on life.

If you are interested in a fasting program, it is probably better to start with a one-day juice fast and work up to a longer regimen. Be sure to follow the guidelines of a health professional any time you fast.

Hair Analysis measures the amount of minerals and heavy toxic metals in the body. For accuracy, the hair is taken from the back of the head, as close to the scull as possible. Some labs can compensate for the effects of dyes or shampoos on the hair itself. Others may not be so reliable. Used in combination with blood tests and urinalysis, hair analysis can be a valuable method of determining your overall health status.

Hypnosis uses the mind to overcome fears or anxieties as well as treating pain and other therapeutic applications, such as sleep disorders, overeating, and smoking and other addictive disorders. If you have a specific medical complaint, or do not feel well, you should have a comprehensive evaluation before undergoing hypnosis.

Massage Therapy was recommended in a Chinese book in 2700 B.C. and has been around ever since. There are several styles of massage therapy; the Swedish is most common in this country. The Eastern style attempts to balance energy paths, while the Western style works on muscles and connective tissue. Massage induces relaxation and helps improve mobility.

Reflexology is a therapy that uses massage and pressure on the hands and/or feet to treat various organs. Based on principles similar to acupuncture or iridology, it is sometimes called zone therapy.

Therapeutic Touch is based on two ancient healing doctrines: Laying-on-of-hands and energy flow. By receiving energy from the healer's hands, the patient's hemoglobin levels can be raised, restoring their vitality.

A CASE STUDY

Be open to new ideas

Even though I've been writing and lecturing on wellness and nutrition more than twenty-five years, I never went to a chiropractor – yes, probably due to some deep prejudice I held that they couldn't help me. Boy were my eyes opened!

I have a balky back and over the years it has given me fits of severe pain, but I always recovered with muscle relaxants and anti-inflammatory prescription drugs-until the fall of 2013. I was in such bad shape I went to the emergency room of a small local hospital. They pretty much said there was nothing wrong and suggested physical therapy "might" help. It didn't.

A month later I was back in the ER, bent over and using a walker to keep myself off the floor. This time they said it was my age and I had to get used to it. I was 69 years old and devastated.

My sweet daughter was so concerned about my poor condition that she insisted I come stay with her and her husband. That evening I was sitting at my computer, and as she breezed by the doorway, she declared, "You're going to Dr. Fogel first thing in the morning. Mike will take you. No discussion about this!"

Dr. Fogel was her family's chiropractor and they had been going to him for years. Since allopathic medicine (what M.D.s practice – also called "traditional medicine") offered no help, I figured I had nothing to lose.

Writhing in pain, hardly able to move my legs, Mike loaded me into his car and took me to Dr. Fogel's office. He was sitting in the reception desk area when I crawled in, took one look at me, and said, "I wouldn't touch you with a ten-foot pole." Then he turned away and picked up the phone.

There's no hope for me I was thinking when Dr. Fogel looked at Mike and said, "Get her to the hospital immediately. They have STAT orders for an MRI."

I was baffled. A chiropractor could order x-rays at a hospital? I was utterly amazed when we arrived at the hospital and I was hurried into radiology. By the time Mike drove me back to Dr. Fogel's office, the good doctor already had my films and was on the phone with the radiologist.

"You're a mess," he said. "You have so many problems – some partially slipped discs, spinal stenosis, bone spurs just to start. Give me twenty weeks and I can fix you."

So, how did it go with chiropractic? Dr. Fogel was wrong – it only took eighteen weeks. He was my miracle worker and he certainly changed my life for the better – much better – and all without pain pills or surgery.

I felt like a fool for waiting most of my life to get the treatment I needed, all because of my prejudice. Please don't do what I did. If one modality doesn't help, open your eyes, and look elsewhere.

Taking care of the human body is an art as old as mankind. There are many, many options for health treatments that have been around for thousands of years, and that fact alone would give them some credibility. Please don't wait until you have a health crisis to seek out advice and treatments from complementary/alternative therapies or practitioners.

GUIDEPOST

Your mind is like a parachute.
It doesn't work if it's not open.

– Frank Zappa

Chapter 8

Physical Therapy

Although in the past physical therapy has been classified an alternative treatment, it's now mainstream and so important we are giving this subject its own chapter. In many cases, PT is an adjunct to other modalities – especially orthopedic surgeries, bone fractures, torn connective tissues, and pain management.

Like other areas of health care, there are *specialist* in PT who are trained to care for certain types of injuries, although their education encompasses all areas of the body. You certainly don't want to go to a PT whose specialty is hands if you have a knee problem. Like other areas of medicine, there are continual changes and advances in PT treatments, and no PT can stay abreast of them all. Make sure your PT is qualified to treat *your* situation. We talked briefly about PT in Chapter 1; here are some more ideas to think about when you start PT:

Facility – is the PT complex logistically appropriate for you? You certainly don't want a long drive as that may inhibit your attendance. Is it clean and efficient? Is the exercise equipment in good working order? Is it cleaned after each patient's use? Do you have to wait for your appointment or do they stay on schedule?

Your Physical Therapist – are their certification and license posted where you can readily see them? Are they appropriately dressed? Do they engage you in conversation and make you feel comfortable? Do they explain everything they do *before* they do it?

Commitment – do you understand that physical therapy takes time and dedication? If you don't *commit* to getting well, you won't. When your PT gives you exercises to do at home, it's up to YOU to do them.

Milestones – some people like to have benchmarks or milestones to achieve so that they can see and feel their improvement. After my shoulder was rebuilt, I made it my goal to lift my arm a quarter inch every day with the over-the-door pulley contraption I was given. You might think that is a puny goal; considering the fact that my shoulder and arm had not moved away from my waist for 17 weeks, one-quarter inch a day was a lot.

Plateaus – more than likely you will reach a point where you don't think there will be any more improvement, even though you are not completely well. Remember that your body has to adjust to its new state of being; if you haven't used a body part in a long while, your body does need time to adapt. Use plateaus to take a deep breath and know that improvement will continue.

GUIDEPOST

Plateaus are platforms for planning and preparation.

Medication – find out from your doctor if it's okay to take an anti-inflammatory prior to your PT sessions. This can help alleviate additional soreness and irritation that can come about in early PT treatments.

Be your own judge – no one knows your limits better than you, so please don't allow anyone to tell you what you *should* be able to withstand and then feel guilty or demeaned because you can't handle that pain or move that joint the way someone else does. We are each a unique person and although there are standards and milestones in recovery, your path will be yours and not the same as the person next to you.

Have you ever heard of or experienced pelvic floor therapy? This is a relatively new treatment for chronic pelvic floor pain, which can be either misdiagnosed as another condition, or possibly not diagnosed at all.[19] Although most common in women, men can also develop chronic pelvic floor pain.

Dr. Eman Elkadry at Harvard Medical School says, "the exact cause of pelvic pain for many women can be elusive, despite lots of tests and scans."[20] Training of gynecologists focuses on organs which may be why muscle problems are overlooked.

The bowl-shaped muscles in your pelvic floor support the bladder, bowel, rectum, and in women, the uterus. When these muscles are too tight, "this causes a condition called myofascial pain,"[21] (Myofascial pain is a muscle pain.). Up to 78% of cases of interstitial cystitis are actually pelvic floor pain according to the *Journal of Obstetric, Gynecologic, & Neonatal Nursing*.[22]

According to the Columbia University Irving Medical Center[23], symptoms can include:

- Bladder incontinence
- Lack of bowel control
- Constipation
- Muscle spasms in pelvis
- Pelvic organ prolapse

Although surgery may be a treatment, in many cases this troubling type of pain can be helped by pelvic floor therapy, which should only be done by a specifically trained practitioner. Dr. Hye-Chun Hur, associate faculty editor of Harvard Women's Health Watch, says that "pelvic physical therapy is normally undertaken by a trained female practitioner."[24]

Since pelvic floor therapy is a highly trained skilled, you should only seek this treatment from a physical therapist who has one of the two certifications of the American Physical Therapy Association (APTA):

CAPP – Certificate of Achievement in Pelvic Physical Therapy at
https://aptapelvichealth.org/

WCS – Women's Health Clinical Specialist at
https://ptl.womenshealthapta.org/

The benefits of physical therapy are cumulative. It takes patience and persistence to restore your mobility and strength. It also requires logical steps, taken in order, and your PT knows every rung on that ladder. Remember, your PT is one of your Guides on your road to recovery. They do not wave a magic wand and make you all better.

How well you do in physical therapy is up to you!

GUIDEPOST

Success doesn't come from what you do occasionally. It comes from what you do consistently.

-InspirationQuotesMagazine.com

Chapter 9

Playing it Safe

During your recovery, pain and limited range of motion will most likely force you into a *play it safe* mode for a while, but as you heal, and start to feel better, you may push yourself into old routines without thinking.

A CASE STUDY

A very sore shoulder

A gentleman I met in physical therapy told me that he was recovering from his second shoulder surgery in six weeks. One surgery was enough for me and I asked him why he had two. After his first rotator cuff repair on his right shoulder, he did exceptionally well and was soon driving.

He was breezing down the freeway one day and, without thinking, stretched his arm to reach for something on the back seat. At that moment, traffic slowed down, and so did he. But the car behind him kept on coming – right into the rear end of his car.

The force of the blow whip-lashed him, with his right arm still behind the seat. All the repairs from the first surgery and weeks in physical therapy were ripped apart.

"It was really stupid," he told me. "I have done that so many times – reach in the back while I'm driving – and I didn't think about it."

Pain and mobility problems can affect other areas of your body, even though they aren't injured or diseased. For example, a bad back can make it difficult to walk; an injured hip or leg causes more stress on the other limb. A neck injury that requires use of a hard cervical collar can make it impossible to turn your head or look down where you are walking.

If you are right handed and injure your right hand or arm, you may tend to be impatient and try to do things you shouldn't be doing. Take your time and do your best to use the other hand.

I was in a hard cervical collar for almost eighteen months, and most of that time I lived alone – in a second story apartment. You better believe that I learned a lot about playing it safe when I was going up and down those stairs. How did I manage?

My twin sister helped me by taking me up and down the stairs several times when I returned home. We counted each step. Then when I was alone, I counted each step, too. I was mindful of each and every time I moved from one level to the next. And, always, always, hold the handrail.

Ordinary chores that a child can do can be unbelievably difficult for someone with an injury. Here are some other ideas to add to your *Play it Safe* arsenal:

1. Don't walk around in socks (you might slip and fall).
2. Always close cabinet doors and drawers.
3. Don't take baths or showers when you are tired (just sponge off and go to bed).

4. Turn on lights at night – be sure outdoor lights are always lit if you are outside. Use night lights, too.
5. Never run to catch your phone – you can always call back.
6. Secure the corners and edges of throw rugs.
7. Don't use a ladder or step stool when you are tired; and when you do use one, make sure your pants legs are neatly tucked into your socks.
8. If you have a bad back, don't sit on soft surfaces. Yes, I know that Lazy-Boy looks comfy; so does that soft, billowy mattress. If you have a bad back, you need *firm support*. You don't have to believe me – ask your doc or your PT. Bad backs need support.

A CASE STUDY

A really dumb accident

My twin sister was very smart, but like all of us, sometimes she did things without thinking. While preparing for a big party at her home, Mary wanted to adjust a balloon bouquet over the breakfast room chandelier. She stood on a chair that has casters (I told you this was dumb), adjusted the balloons (they were perfect) and started her dismount.

Unfortunately, she was wearing long, loose-leg pajamas and the material caught on the armrest of the chair. With the jerk of her leg to loosen the hang-up, the chair scooted across the floor. Backwards she fell, hitting her upper right arm on the stone countertop, landing on the floor. The fracture was so bad that the EMT's had no idea how to lift her off the floor. She was on her back and her elbow was pointing to the ceiling.

Needless to say, the party was cancelled and Mary's arm was never quite the same.

PRESCRIPTION DRUGS

Since there are so many problems with prescription drugs, I am giving you a list of a few things to be aware of:

Drug Interactions   Make sure that your doctor and your pharmacist know all the drugs you are taking as well as any supplements or herbs so potentially harmful interactions can be avoided.

Know what you are taking   Do you know what your doctor prescribed? Can you and your pharmacist read the prescription and dosage? What is that drug for? What are the potential side effects? Are there any interactions with particular foods or beverages?

Is it the right drug?   According to the Massachusetts College of Pharmacy & Allied Health Sciences, 88 percent of errors related to drugs were either the wrong drug and/or wrong dosage.[25]

Allergies?   Are you allergic to any drugs? Have you had side effects from any drugs? If so, your doctor and your pharmacist need to know. Don't be shy about sharing this vital information.

Is it Liquid?   Liquid medicines can be hard to measure; if you need a special device, such as a syringe marked with dosages, be sure you get one and know how to use it.

Because drugs are so important, I am including more information for you in Appendix B.

A CASE STUDY

Odyssey of the Pill and the Patch

From my perspective, one quite common problem is drug interactions, so let me give you another true-life example. I was prescribed two meds for post-op nausea – a scopolamine patch on my mastoid bone behind my ear and Phenergan, a pill.

When my chest started to hurt and breathing became difficult, instinct told me to remove the patch. I did – with the immediate result of projectile vomiting. Later that day at my surgeon's office for a routine follow-up, his PA was very annoyed that I had removed the patch and was still having nausea. I explained my theory, that there may have been a drug interaction, and be became furious – until he pulled out the good old PDR (*Physician's Desk Reference*) and learned that scopolamine *should never* be prescribed with Phenergan.

My patient advocate girl friend asked why no one had checked my chart to see what all had been prescribed (one drug given by the surgeon and the other by the anesthesiologist), and the PA became even more irate. He yelled at my friend that she was making unfair accusations and stormed out of the room.

Her question was perfectly sensible. If a lay person would think to ask this, why didn't the doctors? Had I continued with both the patch and the pill Lord only know what might have happened. Last time I checked, being able to breathe is kind of necessary for life. I could have become just another drug fatality instead of a writer.

To play it safe, you need to be mindful of what you are doing and how you are doing it. Know what drugs you are taking and be alert to any side effects. Don't ignore any symptom of a drug reaction or interaction. Like me, and my mom, your life may depend upon it.

Be careful. We want you to get well.

> GUIDEPOST
>
> Safety isn't expensive
> – it's priceless.
>
> -Unknown

SECTION TWO

THE MIND & EMOTIONS

Chapter 10

Think Positive

Did you know that your thoughts affect your body? It's true – whatever you are thinking does impact the way your body responds and ultimately how it will feel. According to *Psychology Today*:

> "thoughts affect neurotransmitters, the chemical messengers that allow the brain to communicate with different parts of itself and the nervous system. Neurotransmitters control virtually all of the body's functions, from feeling happy to modulating hormones, to dealing with stress. Therefore, our thoughts influence our bodies directly because the body interprets the messages coming from the brain to prepare us for whatever is expected."[26]

The Jed Foundation website says this about being positive:

> "Positivity is the ability to meet challenges and situations in life with an *I can do it, I'll figure it out, things will work out* attitude. People who use the power of positivity face the same disappointments, challenges and stressors in life that everyone does – the difference is that they choose to react to these challenges by finding a productive and positive way to cope and respond."[27]

Since your thoughts *do* affect your body, I hope you can understand that being in a positive frame of mind will yield a better outcome for you. I know from experience that this one step on the road to recovery can also be the hardest. So, let's explore the mental and emotional side of your situation to help you *Think Positive* and feel better.

The first thing to realize is that it is perfectly normal to have a variety of emotional reactions to a trauma – whether it is from illness or accident. Dr. Patti Levin[28] has excellent information on her website and here are some of the emotional reactions to trauma that she includes:[29]

- Grief, disorientation, denial
- Irritability, outbursts of anger
- Emotional swings – crying and then laughing
- Nightmares
- Flashbacks – feeling the trauma is happening now
- Feeling helpless
- Tendency to isolate
- Concern for burdening others
- Depression

- Resurfacing of past unpleasant memories
- Thoughts of suicide
- Desire for revenge

There are numerous coping mechanisms for these conditions; in my opinion, however, the very first strategy you need is to *Think Positive*. I say this because, regardless of the other methods you may use to cope with your situation, if you are not in a positive frame of mind, you're not going to have a positive outcome. How can you be positive when things are looking so dire and your pain is so bad? How do you get yourself into a positive mindset? How do you learn to self-regulate your emotions and feelings?

EVALUATE YOUR WAY OF THINKING

According to The Mayo Clinic, "If the thoughts that run through your head are mostly negative, your outlook on life is more likely pessimistic."[30] If you want to know if your self-talk is negative, Mayo suggests you identify this trend by asking yourself:

1. Do you filter out the positive aspects of a situation and magnify the negative?
2. Do you blame yourself when something bad happens, even if it was not in your control?
3. Do you anticipate the worst when one little thing goes wrong?
4. Do you see everything as bad or good, with no middle ground?

After you analyze your thoughts you can start to change them:

Eliminate all the negative things that can drown out an optimistic outlook::

- Dreary news on tv or radio – politics, weather, pandemic reports, economy
- Negative people and nay-sayers
- Magazines that dwell on everything that's *wrong with you* (weight, age, skin, etc., etc.)

On his *Positivity Blog*[31] Henrik Edberg lists suggestions that I am are summarizing here to help you get onto the positive track:

- Look for something positive in every negative situation
- Ask yourself "What is the opportunity in this situation?"
- Take things slowly to calm your mind and your body
- Don't turn molehills into mountains
- Use the words STOP or NOPE when your mind starts churning out negative thoughts
- Breathe – get quiet and focus on your breathing
- Refocus – ask yourself "Will this matter in five weeks, or five years?"
- Do not allow fears and self-doubt to overtake you; ask yourself, "honestly, what is the worst that could happen?"[32]

- Add value to someone else's life – even if it's just a phone call to say, "Hi, how are you?"
- Smile at yourself in the mirror every morning
- Be mindful – pay attention to what you are doing and how you are doing it

Being Grateful is your next step on the path to being positive. Being negative and being grateful cannot exist in the same space, so when you choose to be grateful, you are purposely putting yourself into a positive place. Gratitude improves both your physical and psychological health and reduces depression.

Applied Psychology: Health and Wellbeing published a study in 2011 that showed that if you spend just 15 minutes before bedtime writing your sentiments about being grateful, that you may sleep better and longer.[33]

So, what does it mean to be *grateful?* The dictionary defines it as "Having a due sense of benefits received."[34] When you are grateful, that means you appreciate what you have now; and when you appreciate *where you are now* you won't worry about what you don't have or what you may have lost, or where you may be going. It's simply a condition of appreciating the moment, the *now.*

Being grateful is so important that the National Institutes of Health (NIH) has research on this subject, saying, "The majority of available research studies indicate that gratitude is associated with an enhanced sense of personal well-being."[35] This site gives numerous examples of the empirical evidence of the connection between gratitude and well-being.

A scale for measuring gratitude has been developed by Dr. Michael E. McCullough and Dr. Robert A. Emmons.

"The Gratitude Questionnaire (GQ-6) assesses a person's gratitude disposition, which is defined as a generalized tendency to recognize and respond with grateful emotion to the roles of other people's benevolence in the positive experiences and outcomes that one experiences."[36]

This simple test only takes a few minutes; if you are interested, here's the link: https://sofia.com.sg/wp-content/uploads/2017/11/The-Gratitude-Questionnaire.pdf

Being positive will go a long way in helping you navigate the Mending Map. Remember these simple rules from the Mayo Clinic:[37]

- *Don't say anything to yourself that you wouldn't say to anyone else.*
- *Be gentle and encouraging with yourself.*
- *If a negative thought enters your mind, evaluate it rationally and respond with affirmations of what is good about you.*
- *Think about things you're thankful for in your life.*[38]

GUIDEPOST

Gratitude is the appreciation of what is valuable and meaningful to oneself and represents a general state of thankfulness and/or appreciation.

-https://www.ncbi.nlm.nih.gov/pmc/articles/PMC3010965/

Chapter 11

Don't despair over setbacks and plateaus

If you are in a situation where you will have a long series of treatments or recovery from an accident or illness, there may be times when you feel as though you can't do any more, or that "this is the best I will get."

Let me assure you are not alone in these feelings and this is not in a unique situation. Many of us who have long-term recoveries have experienced not only setbacks, but also plateaus – those times when we seem to make no progress at all and nothing is getting better. I was in rehabilitation for one month shy of three years after I busted my neck and shoulder in a fall at the headquarters of Turner Broadcasting in Atlanta and most of the ideas in this book came from that situation.

We talked about *being positive* in the last chapter and now is the time to put that skill to use. It's time for you to be your best friend and companion on recovery road.

- ❖ *You* are the only person who can take the treatments.
- ❖ *You* are the only person who can do the physical therapy.
- ❖ *You* are the only person who can control your thoughts.

In Chapter 8 we talked about reaching plateaus in our physical therapy – when our body is adjusting or adapting to its recovered strength or mobility. But setbacks and plateaus can impact all areas of your recovery, not just your PT and sometimes we need to stop before we can move forward.

If the traffic light turns red and brings you to a complete standstill, use that time to reset your radio (clear your mind), adjust your seat (shift your consciousness), and glance in the rear view mirror (to see how far you have come). When the light turns green again, you're ready to move on.

At the beginning of your journey back to wellness, you may have had a good, positive attitude, thinking *this isn't so bad; I can do this*. But dealing with day to day situations such as meals, finances, and family can all make you feel that you have *reached your limit, you can't go on,* or *you can't do it anymore*. It's at times like this when you should stay *positive* and then apply a different set of coping skills.

Motivational Coach, Bob Proctor, says, "There is no good or bad situation – only the meaning we give it." This may sound harsh, unsympathetic, or unrealistic, but let's give this idea some consideration.

Dr. Wayne Dyer said, "What we think about expands." When I first read that, I thought it was ridiculous. Why would a thought "expand." The more I thought about it, the more I thought about it. Until, suddenly, I realized that I was experiencing *exactly* what Dr. Dyer said. He was right. What we think about expands. In other words, we get what we think.

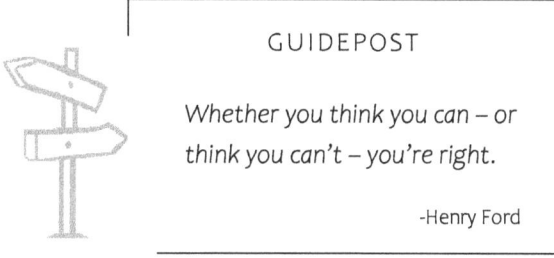

> **GUIDEPOST**
>
> *Whether you think you can – or think you can't – you're right.*
>
> -Henry Ford

When times are tough, it's normal to have negative chatter in our minds because we are programmed this way for protection – our brains process negative thoughts ten times faster than positive thoughts. You better believe that if that tiger gets any closer, all you will think about is running – not about what you'll be eating for lunch tomorrow.

For the sake of discussion, let's say that you have a broken arm and have lost the use of one hand. Not only are you in terrible pain from the fracture, you are constantly thinking about that hand:

> Will I ever use my hand again?
> Will it ever get better?
> How will I ever work again?
> How will I pay my bills?
> How will I drive my car?
> How will I show my children how to tie their shoelaces?
> Will…will…will…???
> How…how…how…???

Do you see what's going on here? You are using your precious thoughts to dwell on ideas that have no value whatsoever. As Coach Proctor says, you are giving negative meanings to a situation with your thoughts that *continue to expand* as Dr. Dyer says. So, what can you do?

Be aware of your thoughts When negative chatter takes over your mind, contributing to those feelings of despair and hopelessness, the first thing you should do is ask yourself:

> What am I thinking?
> Why am I thinking that?
> Does that thought make me feel better?
> If it's not making me better, why am I thinking that?
> What am I doing to myself with these thoughts?

American poet Maya Angelou said, "If you cannot make a change, change the way you have been thinking. You might find a new solution." This is wise advice for anyone dealing with despair.

Once you are *aware* of your thoughts, you can reframe and redirect them – and this does not have to be a difficult or complicated task.

A CASE STUDY

Why are you procrastinating?

I was talking with a mentor about the problems I was having with my recovery; I was in a deep state of despair, and I told her that people kept saying to me: *You'll feel better soon* – or – *you'll be better tomorrow*. And I was really sick and tired of people saying to me, *Cheer up*. There was nothing I wanted more than to cheer up!

My wise mentor asked me, "Do you think you'll get better?"

"Yes," I answered. "My doctors say I can."

"And you are aware that your constant thoughts about your pain, your despair and your set-backs are all delaying your recovery?" she asked.

I had never quite looked at my situation from that view. "Yes," I finally responded.

Then she said something that forever changed my outlook: "Then what are you waiting for? Why are you procrastinating?"

Why was I procrastinating? That simple question changed my recovery and my life – and it can work for you, too. As soon as I was *aware* of my thoughts, I was able to *reframe* them and *redirect them*. I knew in my heart that I *was* going to get better – so, what was I waiting for?

Another lesson for overcoming obstacles and set-backs came from my Mom; she always said, "Take one step at a time." Realize you can't do it all today, but you can take that first step toward tomorrow. Some additional but simple methods for ridding yourself of despair are offered by Colin Falconer[39,40] and paraphrased here:

> **Breathe** – you must do this anyway; just focus on your breathing – in, out; inhale, exhale; repeat.

> **Remember – all things must pass**. Life is constantly changing. *The tide will come back in; it always does.* Until then, keep breathing.

Be gentle with yourself when you think the worst is behind you and then you find yourself back in the pits again. *That's okay, that's how it works.* Go back to step 1 and breathe.

To summarize our talk about despair, I want to share what author, speaker, and yogi Jan Tucker[41] says:

> *No matter how bad life seems, you can find the way out of despair. We all need time to rejuvenate, so break your pattern. Take time to reflect on what you truly want out of life and what you must do to get back on course.*
>
> *The answers often are not complex. They're just hidden because you lost your focus on what's important.*
>
> *Take some time to think about the thoughts or actions that may have led to your despair. Once you identify the problem, with a little guidance you can correct it and completely change your life.*
>
> *The best part? Your answers will often arise on their own once you devote time to yourself to heal and reflect.*[42]

GUIDEPOST

When you pierce the veil of despair, new light can come in.

- Courtney Bowen

Chapter 12

Let go of stress and pain

We are talking about both stress and pain in this chapter because the two are tightly bound to one another. Stress can intensify your pain, and likewise, pain can amplify your stress. That's a double whammy and we need to take care of both.

This may shock you – Pain is neither good nor bad. It's simply Mother Nature's way to get your attention. If you get a splinter in your foot, but don't feel it, and keep walking on it, you're going to have a bigger problem than that splinter. You may develop an infection that's so bad you can't walk. If you don't think that is likely to happen, talk to the diabetic patient who lost their foot because they had neuropathy so bad they didn't feel that splinter. As a result of that infection, they lost their foot. I know that person – she was my sweet sister-in-law. She would have loved it if she had had pain to warn her of that splinter; so please don't hate your pain – it's there for a reason.

Remember our discussion about the mind and its effect on our bodies in Chapter 10? Neuroscientists at Wake Forest University School of Medicine did some interesting research and showed that patients respond to pain according to how much they *think* it will hurt.[43] "The benefit (of less pain) was all in their minds: MRI scans revealed that pain-processing areas in the brain registered less activity when expectations were low."[44]

Lead researcher Robert C. Coghill, PhD suggests that you can lower your expectation of pain prior to a procedure, such as dental surgery, "by telling yourself that you will feel some pain — but it won't be severe."[45] If by chance the pain is more than anticipated, say, "This will only hurt for a little while," and then shift your attention elsewhere. (More on shifting your attention in Chapter 16.)

There are different causes of pain and everyone feels pain differently. For that reason, you should not compare your pain to that of someone else with the same situation – injury, surgery, or illness. Pain not only comes in various levels (from 0 to 10 is a common scale), but it offers you a variety of forms: aching, burning, cramping, jabbing, pinching, stabbing, shooting, stinging, sore, throbbing, and tingling to name a few.

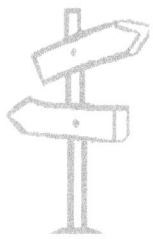

GUIDEPOST

Keep a stress ball handy. Medically speaking, when stress shoots adrenaline into the bloodstream that calls for muscle action; squeezing something provides a release that satisfies our bodies' "flight or flee" response.

-Vatche Bartekian
Askmen.com
How to relax

Although there are basically two classifications of pain - acute and chronic – with the exception of pharmaceutical drugs, both can respond well to alternative, holistic, or natural therapies. If you have just had major surgery, you'll certainly want a powerful pain med such as opioids or morphine; however, you would never take those drugs for a chronic pain.

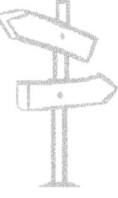

GUIDEPOST

Pain is shocking to your system both physically and emotionally. Once you understand it, you can be the one in control, not the pain.

-Brett Bara

Whereas physical pain originates in the body from injury, illness or surgery, stress originates in the brain and is a result of our thoughts and how we respond to challenges, events, situations. Without a certain amount of stress, we would not survive because it is the flight or fight response to danger (stress) that dumps cortisol, epinephrine, and norepinephrine into our bodies and prepares us for action. So, like pain, stress does have a useful purpose. But excess persistent stress can increase pain and make you depressed. Although we will never rid ourselves of stress, you can learn to control it – both physically and mentally – by the way you react to it.

It's important to get a grip on your pain as soon as possible so that it doesn't become chronic – a pain that lingers long after healing from an injury or surgery. According to the CDC, more than 15% of our population has chronic pain.[46]

Dr. Jenna Walters at Vanderbilt University Medical Center says that "stress or a hectic lifestyle can also push pain levels higher."[47]

So, other than drugs, what are some good ways to deal with pain? Three of the best (in my opinion) are affirmations, meditation, and visualizations. These are so important I'm giving them plenty of space – in Chapter 13. Here are some other ways to treat pain:

TENS unit A Transcutaneous Electrical Nerve Stimulation unit is a powerful, non-drug way to deal with both acute and chronic pain. By flooding the nervous system with electrical impulses, transmission of pain signals to the spinal cord and brain are reduced.[48] Endorphins – your body's natural pain relievers – are also stimulated by the TENS unit, giving you a natural relief from your pain.

I have used a TENS unit with amazing results. So did my twin sister after a severe arm fracture and my next door neighbor, following 12 hours of back surgery. We all found great relief. The nice thing about TENS is that you, the patient, control the frequency and duration of the treatments. TENS units are quite expensive, although some cheaper models are now available. Insurance usually covers the cost if it is prescribed by your doctor. If you have long-term pain, I highly recommend it.

Arnica In my opinion, this herb is an unsung hero in the fight for pain relief. Also known as wolf bane, mountain tobacco, and leopard's bane, it can be effective in treating swelling, bruising, and has some antibacterial properties, although data on humans is lacking.[49] On two separate occasions I have had arnica prescribed by medical doctors.

The first time was by my ophthalmologist who told me I *had* to take arnica pills for two weeks prior to eye-lid surgery. He told me exactly what I needed and told me to order it from Amazon! I was incredulous, but did as he ordered and took them exactly as prescribed. The pills were taken sublingually (under the tongue) and were very pleasant tasting.

The day of my surgery, my daughter insisted that my surgeon give me "real pain pills" when she saw the condition of my eyes – both lids were cut open from the inside next to my nose, all the way to the outer edge. We picked up the drugs on the way home from the hospital and I never took one pain pill – not a single one. Following the good doctor's orders, I continued to take the arnica for several weeks. I had practically no swelling, very little bruising under one eye, and virtually no pain.

Needless to say, when another medical doctor *prescribed* arnica pills and gel for serious chest contusions after a fall, I didn't hesitate.

Like all herbs, it should only be taken with proper medical oversight. If you are on warfarin or another blood thinner, you should not take arnica or use the gel[50] Pregnant or lactating women should also avoid it, as well as people with ragweed, marigold, or sunflower allergies.

Focus on something else If you have ever taken care of a two year old having a temper tantrum, you probably know that the easiest way to get them to quiet down is *distraction*. When you get them to shift their attention away from whatever caused the tantrum, the tantrum ceases. You can do the same with pain! In 1890, the famous psychologist William James published his research on "the relationship between selective attention and experience, profoundly observing *'my* *experience is what I agree to attend to.'"*[51] Research by cognitive psychologists has confirmed that "what we think and feel is determined by what we pay attention to."[52]

If you recall, in Chapter 10 we talked about the benefit of thinking positive when we *refocus*. The same skill can be applied to how we handle pain. The more we think about pain, the more we will hurt, because that's what we are giving our attention to. When you make the conscious choice to think about something other than your pain, you can ease your pain without using toxic drugs. In Chapter 16 you'll find more information on how to make this shift.

CASE STUDY

Find something else to do

If you will indulge me, I'd like to share another personal story which applies to this topic. After my fall at Turner Broadcasting I had surgery to repair my shoulder and was in a hard cervical collar for spinal injuries. The collar went from beneath my lower lip down to my sternum in the front, and from the middle of my head to my shoulder blades in the back. Needless to say, I could not look down nor to either side. Of course, I was in extreme pain, all day long, every day.

The week before I fell, I had signed a contract with a couple who were the subjects of an MGM motion picture (*At First Sight*) because they wanted their "real" story told – not just the movie portrayal which was not entirely accurate. Needless to say, I was in a dilemma about fulfilling my obligations on that contract; besides, I needed the money since I no longer had a job at Turner. The couple was gracious and gave me an extension for my surgery, but I had to get back to work. It was time to refocus; it was time to quit procrastinating.

With only one hand, I sat at my computer every moment I could, typing, typing, typing; reading my research, spending hours and hours talking with the couple. Without realizing it at the time, *I was refocusing* – shifting my attention away from my pain and onto my work. Although we missed the book launch when the movie premiered, I was only six weeks late on delivery.

During those months of writing, I never took a pain pill, although I did take anti-inflammatories. I still had to do home PT six times a day, and three times a week at the clinic. I now use that refocus skill frequently. Believe me when I tell you: It works!

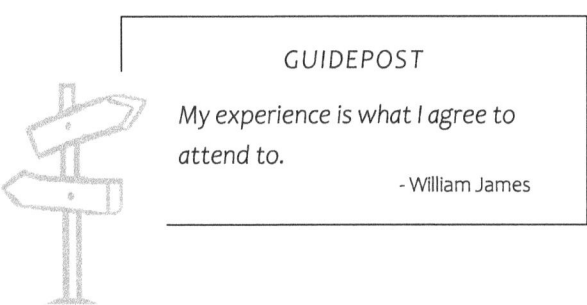

GUIDEPOST

My experience is what I agree to attend to.

- William James

Breathe deep and relax You have to breathe anyway, so why not use this essential function to help control your pain? Inhale deeply and slowly, being sure to expand your abdomen, not your chest. You can put your open hands over your abdomen to be sure they are moving outward as you inhale. If your abdomen is not moving, you're not really taking a deep breath.

Hold the breath for a few seconds and then slowly exhale. Some gurus say you should always breathe out through your nose while others insist it's more effective if you exhale through your mouth. Try and see which works best for you.

The key to this exercise is to say an inspiring or pleasant affirmation to yourself as you inhale (peace, comfort, joy, blessed, etc.) and then release the opposite feeling on your exhale (pain, tension, stress, despair, etc.)

Let's give this a try:

> Breathe in deeply, saying to yourself,
> *I breathe in comfort.*
> Exhale slowly, saying to yourself,
> *I release pain.*

Now you are ready for the next step. Relax comfortably for ten to twenty minutes, and focus only your breathing. Unwanted thoughts will disrupt this process (they always do, so don't think you are doing something wrong), and when this happens *be aware* that you have been distracted and tell yourself to "refocus." Then get back to breathing in those good thoughts and exhaling all that bad stuff.

Commit to do something for someone else Obviously, when you are laid up and recovering from injury, illness, or surgery, you can't take on a commitment that requires physical exertion, but there are plenty of bed-bound activities to keep your mind busy.

- ✓ **Be a mentor** – young people need mentors to help them in their career choices. The guidance and advice you can provide from the comfort of your bed can be invaluable to someone just starting out. Network on FaceBook to find groups in your area of expertise, profession, or hobby and offer to mentor. With Skype and FB chat, you can communicate with people all over the world without spending any money.

- ✓ **Make phone calls** – volunteer to make phone calls for your local politician running for office, or contact charities and find out if you can make donation solicitation phone calls for them.

- ✓ **Write content** – if you like to write, offer to write articles for newsletters of charitable organizations. If you are familiar with non-profits, offer to write applications for grants.

- ✓ **Tutoring** – are you an expert in a particular area of business? Call local high schools, trade schools or colleges and ask if they have a tutoring program.

- ✓ **Sewing & knitting** – do you have sewing or knitting skills? Local hospitals and nursing homes frequently use hand-made caps and shawls for patients. When my twin sister was hospitalized for leukemia, she received a beautiful hand-knit shawl that was so comfortable, she wore it every day.

You will find that when you immerse yourself in doing something for someone else, you won't pay attention to that pain. Here is a link to virtual volunteer opportunities. Who knows – maybe a click of the mouse is all you need to feel better:

https://www.volunteermatch.org/virtual-volunteering

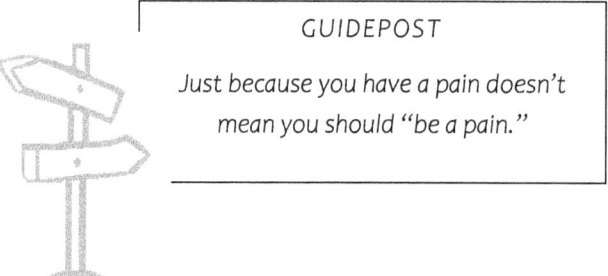

GUIDEPOST

Just because you have a pain doesn't mean you should "be a pain."

In utilizing some of the prior suggestions, it's very important to *not* get stressed out trying to do them. We don't want stress to overcome these coping mechanisms, so let's take a look at stress and some ways to prevent or control it. Like pain, stress can be either acute or chronic[53]. Acute stress can serve us well when we are in imminent danger – remember that *fight or flight* response? Chronic stress, which we are talking about here, is long-term and can last weeks or months.

Eat Well We've already talked about the importance of diet in healing, so this is just a gentle reminder. According to Dr. Mark Hymen, "eating whole, real foods restores balance and reduces the effects of stress on your body."[54] Because your brain and your gut are in constant communication, the good food you eat does have a direct relationship on your stress.[55]

Sleep As we discussed in Chapter 5, you need plenty of shut-eye to help prevent stress – and pain! Check out the list on page 44 for foods to either eat or avoid for good sleep.

Breathe It seems like this word keeps showing up – so it must be important. When you make conscious choices to 1.) be aware of your breathing, and 2.) to concentrate on each breath, you can have a positive impact on your life, and reduce or eliminate both stress and pain.

Socialize Communication with family and friends can help you deal with the throes of your situation – but please don't overdo your complaining or go on and on about your condition. Remember – you get what you think about, or talk about. Be a courteous and mindful listener and don't dwell on your problems. Just absorb the love and kindness they offer and be grateful for their attention.

Smile It's true that a smile lowers stress;[56] it's also contagious. Spread some joy.

Be positive Reflect on the skills in Chapter 10. You can't control everything or everybody in every situation. Let go of negativity so there will be room for the positives.

When you let go of the stress and pain of your illness or injury, you have made good progress toward your destination on *The Mending Map*.

GUIDEPOST

A diamond is just a piece of coal that handled stress exceptionally well.

-Facebook.com/Prince Ea

Chapter 13

Affirmation, Meditation, Visualization

We have talked about the power of the mind over the body and this is nowhere more evident than in visualizations, meditations, and affirmations. We know that our thoughts *do* affect our DNA[57], which means that if we control our thoughts we can channel them to various parts of our bodies and initiate healing. This may sound farfetched if you are not familiar with creative visualizations, meditation, or affirmations, but I can attest from numerous personal experiences that these techniques really do work.

Dr. Linda E. Carlson lead a group of researchers in Canada who studied women who had breast cancer and also participated in *mindfulness meditation* and had support group involvement. Their research, published in *Cancer* in 2014, showed that these women had "preserved telomere length."[58]

> "Telomeres are stretches of DNA that cap our chromosomes and help prevent chromosomal deterioration -- biology professors often liken them

to the plastic tips on shoelaces. Shortened telomeres aren't known to cause a specific disease per se, but they do whither with age and are shorter in people with cancer, diabetes, heart disease and high stress levels. We want our telomeres intact."[59]

This Canadian study seems to ratify 2008 research by Dr. Dean Ornish related to men with prostate cancer[60], adding to the wealth of data on the effectiveness of *mind over matter*. Before we get further into this topic, let's define the terminology of these methods since they all affect the brain but in different ways:[61]

Affirmation – is the use of positive statements to help you overcome negative thoughts. Repeated frequently, you believe them and this helps you make the positive changes you desire.[62] Think of affirmations as exercises for your mind.[63]

Meditation – is the practice of sitting quietly, in state of rest, with "no effort to control our thoughts, breath, or any other aspect of our experience."[64] Meditation moves the mind into the fourth state of consciousness "the realm of being."[65] We use meditation to calm the nervous system.

Visualization / Guided Imagery – is the practice of actively guiding your mind to the outcome you desire, essentially reprogramming your nervous system.[66] In visualizations, all your senses are involved. This practice is used by athletes around the world.

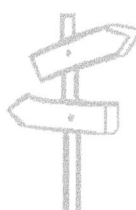

> **GUIDEPOST**
>
> *I never hit a shot, not even in practice, without having a very sharp in-focus picture in my head.*
>
> -Jack Nicklaus, quoted in Psychology Today on-line 12/3/2009 by AJ Adams

When we are injured or ill, we know that we must think in positive terms if we want positive results, and affirmations, meditation, and creative visualizations can all work together to help us.

AFFIRMATIONS

— from the Latin *affirmare*, affirmation means to strengthen or make steady.67 By translating our thoughts into words, and our words into actions, we can manifest our intentions.68 Affirmations can reprogram our brains because they raise the level of hormones that make us feel good so that positive thoughts replace the negative.

Jennifer Williamson has some excellent affirmations for health on her website, <u>HealingBrave.com</u>, which include these:[69]

- I am worthy of good health.
- I am open to new ways of improving my health.
- My body knows how to heal itself. I allow the intelligence of my body to move my health forward.

The Mending Map

My personal favorite affirmation came from Mary Kay Ashe, whom I met in 1972. She said:

Every day in every way I'm doing better and better.

When I was dealing with serious neck and shoulder injuries, I put sticky notes all over my apartment with this affirmation. I could not go from one room to another without seeing this affirmation. I probably said it hundreds of times, if not thousands, during my three-year recovery.

The nice thing about affirmations is that you don't need a quiet place or alone time to say them. You don't need to get into a meditative state. Just say them consistently and watch the change!

Please be aware of your wording in affirmations and never use words such as *want, need, crave, require, must, demand, beg*. Remember, we use affirmations to entice positive thoughts and outcomes. When you use a word such as *want*, you are creating a "want" for yourself. If your say, "I want good health," you are putting yourself into a state of "wanting." By saying that you "want" good health, that implies that you don't currently "have" good health. Even if you are in poor health, you will never get out of that condition by continuing to "want" good health.

GUIDEPOST

We need a new paradigm in health... it begins with the knowledge that the mind and the body can and do heal themselves.

-Robert D. Willix, Jr., MD
FACSM

MEDITATION

– from the Latin *meditari*, meditate means to contemplate, devise, think, or ponder. Historians believe that meditation has been used since 3000 BCE[70] although earliest documented records are from India around 1500 BCE. Meditation can result in some significant benefits to your brain:

1. The **frontal lobe**, the highly evolved part of your brain that handles reasoning, emotions, planning and self-awareness, "tends to go off-line."[71]

2. Activity is slowed in the **parietal lobe**, the area of your brain that orients you in time and space and processes your surroundings.[72]

3. The flow of sensory information of the **thalamus** is slowed to a trickle.[73] The thalamus acts as the gatekeeper for your senses by constantly funneling sensory data deep into your brain. Meditation calms this area of the brain.

4. The **reticular formation**, your brain's sentry, signals your alertness and prepares you to fight or flight. Meditation calms the signal.[74]

Weakening all these neural pathways is not detrimental because you actually lessen your anxiety about distressing or upsetting situations, which is a big Plus! According to Belle Beth Cooper, "When you experience pain, rather than becoming anxious and assuming it means something is wrong with you, you can watch the pain rise and fall without becoming ensnared in a story about what it might mean."

Andy Puddicombe describes meditation this way:

> *Most people assume that meditation is all about stopping thoughts, getting rid of emotions, somehow controlling the mind, but actually it's much different than that. It's more about stepping back, seeing the thought clearly – witnessing it coming and going – without judgment, but with a relaxed, focused mind.*[75]

In addition to lessening anxiety, improving attention and immunity, fighting addictions, improving sleep, decreasing blood pressure, and controlling pain,[76] research also indicates that meditation strengthens creativity and feelings of compassion, while also improving the gray matter of your brain.[77]

The fact that meditation improves your brain's gray matter is one awesome benefit!

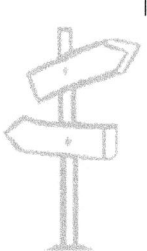

> **GUIDEPOST**
>
> *Your mind is your instrument.*
> *Learn to be its master,*
> *not its slave.*
> —Remez Sasson

How do we meditate? Mindworks.org suggests that you "Just jump in — the moment you do, you will open the door to all of the benefits of meditation."[78]

- Set aside a time, keep it simple, and make it routine. Many people prefer to meditate first thing in the morning; I personally prefer late afternoon.

- You are your own guide. Don't set a time limit – start with just a few minutes.

- Use the deep breathing and relaxation techniques we talked about in Chapter 12 (page 101).

- Don't worry about intruding thoughts – they will come; just re-center yourself.

- Don't give up – and remember the benefits. You won't have results in one session; the key to meditation is consistency.

There are numerous on-line training courses if you want more guidance:

- Mindworks.org
- Mindful.org
- Zenhabits.net
- Gaiam.com
- Shape.com

Meditation is a powerful tool and your experiences with it will be personal to you, so please don't think you need to compare your meditation to someone else's. When used consistently, you will reap the many benefits of meditation.

VISUALIZATIONS / GUIDED IMAGERY

To understand how and why visualizations work, it might help to know a little about your subconscious mind and conscious mind.

According to Abigail Brenner, M.D.,[79] the **subconscious mind** is a programmable hard drive which receives downloaded data from our stimulus-response behaviors. The subconscious mind cannot differentiate between that which is real and that which is imagined since it does not depend on the outside world for its data. Everything is literal and in present time to the subconscious mind, so it will believe whatever you tell it. Because the subconscious mind communicates with feelings and imagination, you can use your mind to practice whatever you desire (hitting a baseball, giving a lecture, stopping a pain) without ever actually doing that particular action.[80]

The **conscious mind** of humans matures and develops over many years and is logical, using words to communicate. As a "thinking" entity, the conscious mind receives its data from the outside world and processes the past and present as well as the future.[81]

Because the conscious mind can be overrun by attitudes, behaviors, and beliefs of the subconscious mind, we must access our subconscious "in order to go beyond our limitations."[82] And that's why creative visualizations are so effective – they allow you to by-pass the limits of the conscious and access the unlimited potentials of the subconscious.

To be successful in your creative visualization you will want to: [83], [84]

1. Desire to actually create what it is you visualize.
2. Be in a relaxed state (meditative).
3. Believe that you will obtain what you visualize.
4. Add as much detail as you can, including your emotions about it.
5. Accept your goal in the visualization and affirm that you are worthy to achieve it.
6. Detach from the outcome and allow the creative process to work its magic.
7. Affirm your visualization throughout the day.
8. Express your gratitude for every step of progress, no matter how small.
9. Repeat on a regular basis.

The set-up for visualizations is like that of meditation although once in your "comfort" place, you will actively engage your mind and all your emotions to envision and "feel" the results you desire.

A CASE STUDY

Balloons and aqueducts

When my neck and shoulder were busted up, my orthopedic surgeon ordered sessions with a psychologist to help me deal with intractable pain and depression. On my first visit with Dr. Schenk he taught me two creative visualizations I will share with you so you'll see how they work. Although they were both for my neck, they were different but effective.

The Mending Map

Your Head is a Balloon – that's what Dr. Schenk said to me after he led me into a meditative state. He told me to envision my head as a balloon, held in place by strings attached to my shoulders. As the balloon slowly rose, it gently straightened my painful neck muscles and nerves, freeing them of crippling pain. This was fine for the muscles and soft tissue injuries, but the serious damage was in my cervical spine and that required its own "treatment."

Your neck is an Ancient Aqueduct – imagine an ancient Roman aqueduct, no longer useable because it is full of corrosion. The water cannot flow freely due to all the obstructions. Dr. Scheck told me to carefully remove the first stone in the aqueduct (the top disc in my cervical spine) and replace it with a brand new, shiny piece of slick PVC pipe. We worked down my cervical spine, replacing all those broken, corroded pipes (discs) with new pieces of piping. When all the pipes were replaced, he told me to envision cool water flowing from the top piece to the bottom, taking all the pain and inflammation away as the water flowed.

After this session, I had immediate relief; it did not eliminate all the pain, but it certainly made it tolerable. Creative visualizations have unlimited applications: heal injuries, sooth aching muscles, knit broken bones, lose weight, improve athletic performance, overcome personal challenges (such as fear of public speaking) – the list is endless. When you put them to use, you'll make good progress on your *Mending Map*.

> ### GUIDEPOST
>
> *I have been visualizing myself every night for the past four years standing on the podium having the gold placed around my neck.*
>
> -Megan Jendrick
> Two Gold Medals Swimmer
> 2000 Summer Olympics

Chapter 14

Don't play the Blame Game

If you don't learn anything else from this book, please remember this:

You can't be bitter and get better at the same time.

When we have a bad accident, caused by someone else, it's very easy in today's litigious environment to file a lawsuit and, in many cases, receive a huge financial windfall. But what is the real price you pay? Is it just "pain and suffering" or is there more?

I'm not saying that you should not receive some sort of compensation for injuries sustained due to the negligence of another, but before you file suit you should consider these factors:

You make yourself a victim
As soon as you file a claim, you become the plaintiff – and to be the plaintiff means you are the *victim*. That makes you the prey or target of the defendant and their attorneys. Be

prepared for them to pull out all their guns to shoot holes in your complaint.

You lose your power

Now that you have filed the law suit, you are dependent upon your attorney, the judge, the jury, and the defendant to set your course. When everything is everyone else's fault, you do not have the power to change it.[85] Are you willing to give them that power?

> **GUIDEPOST**
>
> The stress of litigation alone may add to the litigant's suffering.
>
> -*Personal Injury and Emotional Distress*
> http://criminal-justice.iresearchnet.com/forensic-psychology/personal-injury-and-emotional-distress/

Distracts from your healing

According to Dr. Larry Strasburger the experience of a law suit "saps energy and distracts the litigant from normal daily preoccupations that we call *life*."[86] Dr. Strasburger also says that litigation distress can cause:[87]

- Sleeplessness
- Anger
- Frustration
- Humiliation
- Headaches

- Difficulty concentrating
- Loss of self confidence
- Indecision
- Anxiety
- Despondency

Note that all of these conditions are symptoms of PTSD.

Loss of Support System

You need the support of family and friends when you are recovering; the demand for even more support during the long process of litigation can cause them to "burn out" leaving you without the help and encouragement your recovery requires.

You become more symptomatic

If you are suing for "diminished capacity" or "permanent injury" the only way you can substantiate your claim is to either stay in that state of injury or become even worse. This is what we call "negative reinforcement."

CASE STUDY

The wheelchair and lots of money

My neighbor was a nursing home administrator and she injured her back one day while trying to catch a resident who was falling. She immediately filed a law suit against her employer and rather than doing physical therapy for her injury, she opted for surgery. She was hurt and she was bound and determined to prove it, even though she was still ambulatory (able to walk). Of course, it was a huge mistake.

The surgery only exacerbated her problem; she is now in a wheelchair. I heard that she received a huge payout – and she will never walk again.

Delays your recuperation
Most law suits are long, drawn out processes that can take years, and during that time the plaintiff's integrity and honesty will be challenged. Giving a deposition has been referred to a "being stripped naked"[88] and the litigant is not able to "move on with their life."[89]

Loss of personal privacy
When you file a law suit, it becomes a matter of public record. You will have to submit to depositions, interrogatories, and public testimony. Every facet of your life will be examined and cross-examined.

Reliving the trauma
Catastrophic accident injuries can cause emotional distress and even PTSD. If you file a lawsuit, be prepared to "relive the accident."[90]

Your personal growth is stunted
When you blame someone, you will constantly spend time defending yourself. This "part-time job"[91] also shuts us "down to what others have to offer us in terms of lessons and growth."[92]

> ## GUIDEPOST
>
> Money does not make people whole.
>
> -R.L. Trimble, M.R. McNeil, DE: *Is money a cure?*:
> follow-up of litigants in England.
> Bull Am Acad Psychiatry Law 19:151-60, 1991

Blame is contagious

The *Blame Game* can bleed over into other areas of your life and you'll find yourself blaming everyone for everything. When this happens, you are relinquishing your personal responsibility for your own actions in other areas of your life. This can also arouse the other party to counter-blame you rather than take responsibility for their own deeds.

If your injuries are the result of egregious acts and a law suit is your only recourse for any sort of restitution, by all means find a reputable personal injury attorney. Just beware of the various consequences we have talked about so that you will be prepared to meet them head-on and win your case.

> **GUIDEPOST**
>
> If your recovery is slow, don't blame your doctor; no two people heal the same and your health professional will be your best ally if you communicate with them properly.

Chapter 15

Keep a sense of Humor

When you laugh, you trigger a wonderful chain of reactions in your body[93]:

- Endorphins are released, lowering blood pressure, which
- Improves circulation, strengthening the cardiovascular system.
- Nervous system is stimulated bolstering the immune system.
- Even your facial muscles get a workout

Best of all, you get all these benefits without using any pharmaceutical drugs!! That's a win-win. In her article, *It's Official – Laughter Lowers Blood Sugar*[94], Hazel Spurr says:

"…it is known that negative emotion such as fear and anxiety can raise blood glucose levels" and she goes on to report that Dr. Keiko Hayashi at the University of Tsukuba in Japan has proven that "Laughter has a positive effect on the neuroendocrine system which suppresses the elevation of blood glucose. The inhibitory effect of laughter on increased post-prandial blood glucose levels suggests the importance of daily opportunities for laughter in patients with diabetes."[95]

> "Always laugh when you can.
> It is cheap medicine."
> -Lord Byron

If laughter can improve a condition that is as complicated as diabetes, just think of what it can do for you. Norman Cousins, a book critic and author, who also did research on the biochemistry of human emotions, said, "I made the joyous discovery that ten minutes of genuine belly laughter had an anesthetic effect and would give me at least two hours of pain-free sleep."[96]

Cousins suffered from painful and debilitating ankylosing spondylitis as well as a collagen (connective tissue) disease. In 1979 he published a book, *Anatomy of an Illness as Perceived by the Patient*[97] in which he writes about his use of "laugh therapy" during his struggles with illness.

His experience was later published in *The New England Journal of Medicine* and gave rise to a new field of medical science: Psychoneuroimmunology[98] which can be defined this way:

> Your thoughts and feelings (**psycho**)
> affect the chemicals in your brain (**neuro**)
> which affect the hormones that fight disease
> (**immunology**)[99]

So, how do you get more laughter into your life:

Watch
    Funny movies
    Old slap-stick comedies
    Sit-coms
    You-Tube - Carol Burnett, I love Lucy, SNL

Read
    Joke books
    Funny blogs
    Pintrest Boards of funny things

Listen
    Tapes by comedians
    Podcasts of funny stories

Laugh at yourself
    How funny is your hair when you first wake up
    Smile, even when you don't feel like it
    Reminisce over funny situations in your life
    Talk nice to yourself
    Laugh at mistakes you make

Laugh with others
    Talk to children
    Play with a pet
    Go to a comedy club

Sometimes laughing at yourself will give you the best laugh of all. When I was recovering from injuries, my three-year old grandson had great fun fastening and unfastening all the various Velcro contraptions that were holding me together – the Aspen collar around my neck, a wrist brace, the shoulder restraint that covered my arm and wrapped around my waist, and knee and ankle braces. One afternoon, he looked up at me and said very sweetly, "You're the Velcro Nana!"

After that insightful opinion of my condition, I could no longer see myself as pathetic – after all, *I was the Velcro Nana.*

This quote is a good way to summarize our talk about the benefits of laughter:

Laughter

Laughter is a melody,
    A concert from the heart
A tickling by the Angels,
    Creative living art.
Laughter heals and comforts,
    It's sometimes gentle – sometimes bold,
Laughter is a freeing dance,
    Performed within the Soul

                        -S. West

Chapter 16

PTSD, EP and EFT – let's get un-stuck

Are you stuck in your recovery? Do you feel like giving up? Are you ready to throw in the towel?

Let's talk about your brain. If your life were a computer, the key board would be the input (every life experience), the processor would be your amygdala (what you saw, felt both emotionally and physically, tasted, touched, learned, heard, believed, etc.) and the storage would be your hippocampus (dates, times, situations, weather, people, place, things, etc.). The amygdala is so essential, that it is fully functioning when you are born; however, the hippocampus doesn't really get to work until we are around two to three years old (which explains why we have no memories of infancy and early childhood).

When you have a highly stressful or traumatic experience, "the amygdala goes into overdrive, pulling in gigabytes of both external environmental information, as well as internal physical-response information."[100] This is a basic protective mechanism – the brain never wants to forget something that might be a danger. During this process, you receive an abundant supply of stress hormones, such as:

- Cortisol
- Adrenalin
- Noradrenalin

Guess what these chemicals do beside preparing you for fight or flight? They pretty much put the kibosh on your hippocampus. Wow – so all that stimulus is input, but it's not properly sorted, dated, and filed. This is a simple explanation for PTSD – you remember the experience, but because it was not "date stamped" you feel like it is happening all over again in the present moment.

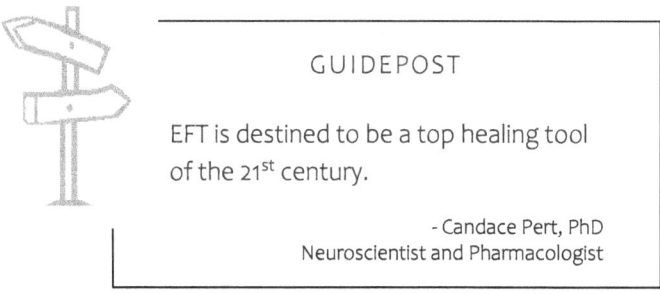

GUIDEPOST

EFT is destined to be a top healing tool of the 21st century.

- Candace Pert, PhD
Neuroscientist and Pharmacologist

If you find that you are still stressed out or in chronic pain, in spite of doing everything you can to get well, you may be referred to a counselor or psychologist to help you deal with these emotional upheavals of your situation. Among the various modalities available to psychologists is a new and very effective treatment that has only been around since the early 1990's. Once you learn the process, it costs you nothing except your time. Although this therapy is embraced by the field of psychology, it is actually a merger of psychology and acupuncture – and is truly a mind-body treatment. This therapy came about because the field of biology is finally starting to update its understanding of how the human body functions based on the principles of quantum physics.[101]

The implications are proving to be as astounding as the innovations of high tech. The basic premise behind this "energy psychology" (EP) is that our negative thoughts, beliefs, and emotions (which are energy) can get stuck in the body and clog up the natural flow of energy. This stuck energy (trapped emotion and pain) is the cause of emotional and physical pain as well as disease.

GUIDEPOST

We are slowed down sound and light waves, a walking bundle of frequencies tuned into the cosmos. We are souls dressed up in sacred biochemical garments and our bodies are the instruments through which our souls play their music.

- Albert Einstein

In traditional psychology patients improve by gaining insight into the causes of their emotional difficulties and learning to change behaviors. This process can be expensive and slow, sometimes taking years or even never.

On the other hand, EP leads the way into 21st century psychotherapy with a rapid, reliable, and lasting treatment for a broad range of physical and emotional issues by applying some of the aspects of quantum physics. A simplified way to think of EP is to view it as *acupuncture for the emotions, but without the needles.* This method has been applauded by renowned physicists like William Tiller, best-selling neuroscientist Candace Pert[102], and scores of medical doctors, psychologists, and psychiatrists who now use EP routinely in their practices.

The modality for EP is called Emotional Freedom Technique, or EFT, and involves tapping on various meridian points around the head, face, and upper body. This tapping with two fingers has been shown to calm the amygdala, that part of your brain that has all that stuck traumatic data.

When we "tap" about our limiting beliefs (*I'm never going to get well*), traumatic memories (*that accident was terrible and ruined my life*), or pain (*this is the worst pain imaginable*), we shift our perspective, gently allowing our subconscious to consider change. Once the subconscious realizes there is nothing to gain from holding on to the problem, it is open to changing.

Please don't think that tapping is some sort of voodoo science. There are hundreds of research projects about this incredible modality, including Harvard Medical School.[103] For a comprehensive list of world-wide research, check out this site:

https://www.thetappingsolution.com/science-research/

Let's talk about some of the BENEFITS OF EFT:

- ❖ It is a simple tool that gives gentle and long-lasting relief.
- ❖ It focuses on energy patterns in the body and often works where standard and even alternative therapies don't.
- ❖ No drugs or special equipment are needed.
- ❖ Anyone can quickly learn EFT, even over the telephone.
- ❖ The tapping doesn't have to be done "perfectly" to work.
- ❖ There is no minimum or maximum amount of tapping.
- ❖ You can tap as little or as often as you want.
- ❖ Emotional problems, as well as physical problems, can be alleviated.
- ❖ You don't even have to believe in this technique in order for it to work.

Although this modality is easy to learn, you should get instruction from a certified EFT practitioner. I usually don't refer people to websites for instructions, but in this case I'm making an exception. The Tapping Solution provides an abundance of credible information and free videos to introduce you to EFT:

www.thetappingsolution.com.

To find a Certified EFT practitioner, visit The Association for Comprehensive Energy Psychology (ACEP) at:

https://www.energypsych.org/search/custom.

Several years ago, I co-authored a book about EFT with Janiece C. Andrews, MD, a psychiatrist at Penn State, and we created our own EFT man. This will show you the various meridian points of the body that are used in tapping.

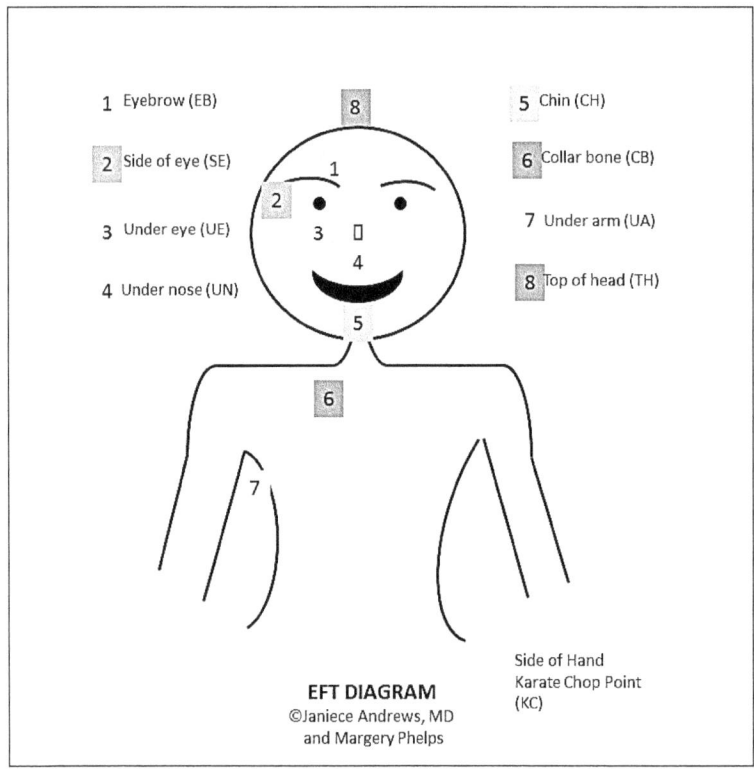

If you are still skeptical about EFT, here are some opinions from medical and scientific professionals:

EFT is a simple, powerful process that can profoundly influence gene activity, health, and behavior.
– Bruce Lipton, PhD

EFT offers great healing benefits.
-Deepak Chopra, MD

The results of EFT, as measured in a multitude of studies, have been astoundingly positive – better, in fact, than the outcomes of any other therapy that has been offered.
-Sue Johnson, Clinical Psychologist

For those seeking a prescription for eliminating limiting, self-sabotaging beliefs that lead to fear, anxiety, and chronic illness, look no further than "The Tapping Solution."
-Lissa Rankin, MD

Put away your skepticism; this really works…I've had great results with tapping in my own life.
Wayne Dyer, PhD

> **GUIDEPOST**
>
> Tapping is one of the most directed and powerful ways to peel away those layers of chronic stress.
>
> -Dr. Mark Hymen

SECTION THREE

THE SOUL

Chapter 17

Stay in touch with your Higher Power

Nonlocal mind is a term coined by Dr. Larry Dossey to describe "the unbounded ways in which consciousness displays itself in space and time."[104] And one of the forms of the nonlocal mind is a word with which we are all more familiar – *prayer*.

According to a publication on The National Library of Medicine website, "Prayer is a special form of meditation and may therefore convey all the health benefits that have been associated with meditation."[105]

To understand why the power of prayer in healing is only in recent times being researched, it might help to understand a little about the history of medical arts.

In his ground-breaking book, *Reinventing Medicine*, Dr. Dossey says that for fifty thousand years shamans "have used expectation and suggestion to help people heal."[106] We know that the ancient religious texts refer to prayer and belief in healing, and as early as the 4th Century BC, "medicine was often practiced by priests"[107] in Babylonia, Egypt, India, and Rome.[108]

For millennia, the healing arts have been greatly impacted by economics, governments, religions, and science[109] with one of the most important events occurring in the 1770's. That's when Rene' Descartes, a French philosopher and mathematician, created scientific dualism, which basically teaches that the mind and the body are separate. "The vital energy which was the God force—once thought to animate all living things—was pushed further and further back."[110]

Newtonian physics and chemistry further denied the existence of "subtle energies" and in the 1930's the mind-body connection was finally dismissed by Western medicine.[111] Thankfully today, with the emergence of quantum physics, we are returning to the idea that the mind, body, and spirit are connected and not separate, but actually three parts of the whole.

> GUIDEPOST
>
> We have made colossal errors in defining ourselves only in terms of the physical body.
>
> -Larry Dossey, MD,
> Reinventing Medicine, pg.206

> "Modern consciousness research reveals that our psyches have no real or absolute boundaries; on the contrary, we are part of an infinite field of consciousness that encompasses all there is—beyond space-time and into realities we have yet to explore."
> – Stanislav Grof [112]

In research about prayer and healing, the matter of consciousness is frequently interjected, but those of us who believe in the power of prayer know that it is actually beyond our consciousness. This radical idea is endorsed by some great minds who certainly have a better understanding of consciousness. Larry Dossey writes:

> "…there is no reason to close the books on the role of consciousness in health. Even if the brain were capable of actually producing consciousness, for which there is no evidence, no one has a clue about how the *contents* of the mind—specific thoughts—would come about as a result. 'No,' Einstein once said in response to this idea, 'this trick won't work…How on earth are you ever going to explain in terms of chemistry and physics so important a biological phenomenon as first love?' His contemporary, Niels Bohr, whose name is synonymous with modern physics, agreed that physics cannot shed much light on the mind. 'We can admittedly find nothing in physics or chemistry that has even a remote bearing on consciousness.'" [113]

> *Prayer is simply a
> two-way conversation
> between you and God.*
>
> -Billy Graham

Prayer differs for every religion – it's meditation for Buddhists, the rosary for Catholics, centering for Protestants, and davening for Jews. Regardless of the name attached to it, prayer is healing because it is basically meditation -- a repetition of words and sounds[114] -- which has been proven by MRI scans to make physical changes in the brain.[115]

Hundreds of studies on prayer have shown numerous benefits of prayer, including: [116]

- Healthier lifestyles
- Helps control pain
- Cope better with illness
- Combat depression
- Improve self-control and relationships
- Turns on genes that fight disease
- Shorter hospital stays

Praying for others has also proven to be effective in many studies, although some research contradicts the findings.

According to Josh Clark, "Prayer is the number one complementary medicine for Americans, more than vitamins, herbs or therapeutic exercise like yoga. If it makes someone feel better -- even if can't be proven scientifically -- what harm does prayer pose?"[117]

I personally believe that we pray because it satisfies our longing (that all people have) to connect with a Higher Power – Source – or God – and that in so doing we are reminded that we are never alone, that there is *something infinite* beyond ourselves, and that we are part of it. Ultimately, it's all a matter of belief.

GUIDEPOST

Is prayer your steering wheel or your spare tire?

-Corrie ten Boom

Lord, make me an instrument of thy peace.
Where there is hatred, let me sow love,
Where there is injury, pardon;
Where there is doubt, faith;
Where there is despair, hope;
Where there is darkness, light;
And where there is sadness, joy.

O Divine Master, grant that I may not so much seek
to be consoled as to console,
to be understood as to understand,
to be loved, as to love.

For it is in giving that we receive,
It is in pardoning that we are pardoned,
and it is in dying that we are born to eternal life.

— St. Francis of Assisi

Chapter 18

Follow your Intuition

We are taught that we have five senses – taste, touch, smell, sight, and hearing – and each of these senses is related to certain organs in our body. In actuality, however, there are other senses we seldom hear about:

> **Vestibular** - our body's perception of gravity, balance, and movement (lying down, standing up, walking a tight rope)
>
> **Proprioception** – knowing where our body parts are, our position in space, and planning movements (such as clapping our hands together, putting a fork full of food into our mouth)
>
> **Interoception** – the physical feelings in your body that tell you what emotion you're feeling (a broken heart, butterflies in your stomach, gut feeling)[118]

Where does this leave *intuition*, commonly referred to as our sixth sense? The fact that science is still finding and defining new senses is testimony that there is much we don't yet know or understand about the human experience. And one of those senses we are still researching and trying to explain is intuition.

We all have intuition but all too often it is either ignored or defiled as being immoral. Have you ever been driving your car and start to change lanes, only to have a "knowing" to stay where you are just as some fool driver cuts in? That's your intuition – your higher self – looking out for you. Some say this is your angel protecting you. Others claim it is just a coincidence.

On the *Psychology Today* website, Francis P. Cholle gives us this definition of intuition:[119]

> *Intuition is a process that gives us the ability to know something directly without analytic reasoning, bridging the gap between the conscious and nonconscious parts of our mind, and also between instinct and reason.*

Terri Britt, former Miss USA, writes about intuition on her website and says, "When we get out of the way with our minds and tune into our higher selves, we tap into God's guidance and love."[120]

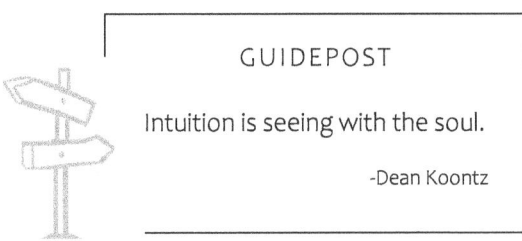

GUIDEPOST

Intuition is seeing with the soul.

-Dean Koontz

So, what does intuition have to do with healing and what guidepost does it provide on our mending map? For one thing, your medical diagnosis may be due in part to intuition. The National Institutes of Health (NIH) has done research of the effects of clinical diagnostics versus intuitive diagnoses and has come up with some very interesting results.[121] Although there are mixed findings and conclusions in some of the research, "In another study, accuracy in interpreting electrocardiograms was found to improve when participants were prompted to use a combination of analytical and intuitive strategies."[122]

Such notable medical professionals as Norman Shealy, MD, (a Harvard trained neurosurgeon), Mona Lisa Schulz, MD, PhD (a neuroscientist and neuropsychiatrist), Judith Orloff, MD (a psychiatrist), and Carolyn Myss, PhD, (an intuitive healer), have all been involved in research regarding intuition and healing.[123] But you don't have to be a medical doctor or PhD to experience the benefits of intuition and healing. Mothers are often times "tuned in" to their children's well-being and can even save their lives.

CASE STUDY

A mother versus the emergency room

A small local hospital's emergency room near my home was notorious for poor care and I was collecting stories about the situation in hopes of getting it remedied. Thankfully, it was sold to a major medical care provider and then closed, so my work was no longer required, but I've never forgotten one story.

An eight year old girl complained of difficulty breathing so her mother and much older sister took the child to that emergency room. With little treatment, she was dismissed with "mild asthma" and sent home. The next day, her breathing was more labored, so they returned to the facility. Again, she was dismissed – no x-rays were taken, even though the little girl's breathing was very troublesome.

On their way back home, the mother said to the older daughter, "I don't feel right. There's something wrong, something bad wrong. Let's get to the children's hospital right away."

On entry to that emergency room the child was swept up, taken to x-ray, and immediately diagnosed with a tumor as big as a grapefruit. Five hours of surgery later, the little girl was expected to make a full recovery. Had that mother not listened to her intuition, they would have been planning a funeral.

Each of us has been endowed with the God-given gift of intuition but when it comes to your health, you would be ill advised to rely solely on your own intuition. By all means seek out proper medical attention – and then allow your intuition (I call mine my *silent voice*) to have its say. To hone your skills of intuition, or to wake them up if they have been long dormant, here are a few things to try:

Be mindful – pay attention to your physical senses; as you become more aware of bodily sensations, you'll realize that there's more going on – that's your intuition.

Meditate – get into your quiet zone, tune out distractions, and ask yourself questions. What do you need to know? If you have a problem, ask for guidance – whether it is physical, emotional, financial. You'll be amazed at the answers you will receive.

Monitor your dreams – when we are asleep and disconnected from our rational/thinking mind, our intuition has the opportunity to speak. Allow it to do so.

Recognize intuition - did you have a certain feeling about a particular situation and then "see" it actually happen? Don't dismiss that feeling; don't ignore it. That was your *silent voice* talking to you. Embrace what it says, listen to it, and learn from it.

Don't limit your intuition - you don't need to be in a meditative state for your intuition to be active because it is always "turned on" and can *speak* at any time (like when that car jumped lanes and almost hit you). Always listen; I've found that my *silent voice* has never misspoken. I always regretted the times I did not listen.

Use Affirmations to reinforce your intuition:

- I trust my inner wisdom.
- My intuition speaks my truth.
- My intuition is a blessing to me in all areas of my life.

The theologian, Florence Scovel said, "Intuition is the spiritual faculty that doesn't explain; it seemingly points the way."[124]

You can use your intuition as one of the guides on your own *Mending Map*.

> GUIDEPOST
>
> The intellect has little to do on the road to discovery. There comes a leap in consciousness, call it Intuition or what you will, the solution comes to you and you don't know how or why.
>
> -Albert Einstein

Chapter 19

Find a Hero

Sometimes when we are recovering from a serious illness or injury it helps if we have someone to emulate – someone we look up to who has had a similar experience, or someone we have personally witnessed in a challenging situation. I call these very special people a *Hero*.

There is no limit to the characteristics of a hero – they can be very young or they can be elderly; they can be financially well off or they can be underprivileged; they can be geniuses or they can be uneducated; they can be physically fit or they can be sickly.

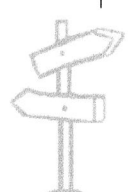

GUIDEPOST

Heroes exceed what is expected of them, they make a positive impact on people's lives, and they rise above and beyond the ordinary.

-Chelsea Chico
Blog.Ricmond.Edu
March 22, 2015

Many people see sports figures as heroes, as someone to imitated; other heroes are soldiers, astronauts, and of course, the police and fire fighters. Anyone we look up to for inspiration can be our hero. So, let me tell you about one of my heroes when I was traveling along the mending map. It was only due to the caring concern of an employee in the HR Department at Turner Broadcasting that I found one of my heroes after a fall in the employee cafeteria.

"I've made an appointment for you to see Dr. Ciepiela," she said to me. "Who?" I asked, having no idea who this man was. During the next two and half years while under his care, I learned more about this doctor, and on my journey he did become one of my heroes. He was a former NFL player for the Bengals, the Oilers, and the Saints. As a free safety, he was involved in lots of dangerous plays, and one of them left him with a broken neck. He was carted off the field, paralyzed, had three neck surgeries, and laid in the hospital for a year.

He told me that one day, after all he had been through, with not much hope of recovery, he felt some tingling in his toes, and then his fingers. He started to believe that he would get well, and did just that. His football career was obviously over and he had to figure out what to do with his life, so he decided to go to medical school. I've had scores of doctors in my life, but Dr. Ciepiela is #1.

When he found out how badly injured my neck was he said, "We're not screwing around with your neck the way they did with mine," and he called in an array of doctors to put me back together – a neurologist, neurosurgeon (don't ever have spinal surgery by an orthopedist), pain specialist, and two physical therapists. He was my hero not only because he rescued me, he was a role model to be emulated.

If he could recover from his paralyzing neck fractures and become a world-class orthopedic surgeon, I could certainly recover from my injuries and get back to writing.

Besides inspiring us, what do heroes really do? According to Scott D. Allison, PhD, in *Psychology Today*, there are "5 Surprising Ways that Heroes Improve our Lives."[125]

1. **Elevation of our emotions** – Thomas Jefferson "used the phrase *moral elevation* to describe the euphoric feeling one gets when reading great literature."[126] Have you ever experienced something that left you with feelings of awe or reverence? Your hero can elicit these same elevations of feelings in you – and we know that positive feelings are a component of wellness.

2. **Soothe our Psyches** - Stories about heroes are "a salve for people's psychological wounds"[127] because they calm fears, lift spirits, and nurture hopes according to Dr. Allison.[128] These comforting stories can help us heal.[129]

3. **Enhance social connections** – our social relationships are amplified when a hero "performs actions that exemplify and affirm"[130] our community values. They become role models "that reinforce our most treasured values and connections with others."[131]

4. **Show us how to transform our lives**[132] - because heroes go through their own transformation on their journey, they show us that we, too, can risk change and transformation in our own lives.

5. **Inspire us to become heroes** – those warm fuzzy feelings of *elevation* which lift us up, can also motivate us to be a better person. Witnessing a heroic act can help us believe that we, too, are capable of doing the same.[133]

Joseph Campbell, who was a professor of literature and mythologist and the inspiration behind *The Star Wars Saga*, gives us this thoughtful summary of heroes:

> *We have not even to risk the adventure alone, for the heroes of all time have gone before us. The labyrinth is thoroughly known; we have only to follow the thread of the hero path. ... And where we had thought to travel outward, we shall come to the center of our own existence. And where we had thought to be alone, we shall be with all the world.*[134]

Chapter 20

Believe you will be well

From the beginning of this book we have talked about our *beliefs* and how they impact our ability to recover from illnesses and injuries and lead us across the mending map to wellness. So, in summarizing our journey together, we want to review and then add to this all important concept.

Dr. Lewis Mehl-Madrona is both an MD and a PhD. He graduated from Stanford University School of Medicine and is board-certified in family medicine and his book, *Healing the Mind through the Power of Story* has some powerful lessons for us and our beliefs.

> GUIDEPOST
>
> *My feeling is that if you don't explore the story behind why you are doing what you are doing then there's a risk you won't maximize your capacity to heal. So why not get the power of the mind behind what you do?*
>
> -Lewis Mehl-Madrona, MD, PhD

According to Dr. Mehl-Madrona, "the story you tell yourself about your illness matters a lot."[135] The ancient idea of a *narrative paradigm* originated with indigenous cultures who believed that everything that really matters is part of a story.[136]

In conventional medicine, the diagnosis is the only thing required because the patient is treated according to that diagnosis. However, when working with illnesses or injuries that require the participation of the patient, such as when the treatment is for chronic or life-threatening situations, "the story is really important because the story tells us what the patient will believe is possible to help the illness."[137]

Notice that Dr. Mehl-Madrona says *what the patient will believe is possible*. What he's saying is that the story you tell yourself will have an impact on the ending of your story! Let's talk about two patients, the first one being from the doctor's book.

A man diagnosed with multiple sclerosis (MS) *believed* he could get well in spite of his neurologist telling him that he *would not* recover. If you believe that "story," it's difficult, if not impossible to recover from MS.

But the man with MS continued to *believe* it was possible, and that's the story he told himself. On a retreat he wrote a story about his illness, and *why* he had gotten sick. Then he asked himself, "how is this helping me?"[138] He went on to make a list of the ways MS had improved his life: he was more compassionate, had more respect for people with mobility problems, greater patience, etc.

Then he thought, "Maybe multiple sclerosis is a guest, and not a permanent dweller in my house. Maybe it came as a spiritual teacher. It's like a houseguest, and when the refrigerator is empty, he'll leave my house. I better talk to it.

When I learn everything it wants to teach me, it will not have reason to stick around."[139]

Eventually, the man felt he had learned everything his disease wanted to teach him and he started to recover, stopping the neurological deterioration of MS, and gaining strength. Continuing in this mindset, by rewriting the story of his illness, he eventually made a full recovery.

This may sound like an extreme example, but it's not; most of us know people who have "miraculously" recovered from serious health challenges. His *belief* and writing his own story about his illness were the cure.

On the opposite end of the spectrum is the patient who believes that 1) they will never get well, or 2) that their recovery is based on *what they do* and not what they actually *believe*. To illustrate, here is our second story:

CASE STUDY

I need to do it perfectly

My neighbor Eva was diagnosed with advanced lung cancer. She had never smoked but a nagging cough for almost a year finally lead to the dire diagnosis. This lady was one of the most spiritually enlightened and loving souls I ever knew, so it baffled me when she started to tell us, "When I get my mind right, the cancer will go away."

We all talked to her about this attitude that she had to *get her mind right*, we had prayer circles, and even laying on of hands; the cancer responded by getting worse. We encouraged her *to believe* she would recover to no avail. Her *belief* was that she had to *think right*. Her belief was that there was something she *had to do*.

Belief is not something you *do*. Belief is something you *have*. You cannot qualify or quantify belief. You cannot put beliefs into a time frame. If it is raining this morning, that is a fact – it is something that you *know*. If you say *Tomorrow it will be sunny* that is a belief. It is our beliefs that impact our health.

Do you see the difference in these two stories? The man with MS desired to get well, so he wrote his story around the premise that his disease had something to teach him, and he actively engaged it in a dialogue through writing, poems, and questioning. Yes, he was *doing* something, but unlike Eva, he approached it with an open mind. He had no preconceived ideas about what the illness would teach him. His *belief* was that when he learned the lessons, he would recover.

Eva, on the other hand never *believed* she would get well. She believed that she would be well IF she *had her thinking right*.

GUIDEPOST

We are never more than a belief away from our greatest love, deepest healing, and most profound miracles.

-Gregg Braden

Many, many years ago a urologist told me that my bladder was no longer functioning and I would be on a leg bag or intermittent catherization (IC) the rest of my life. I was thirty-eight years old and decided that I did not want to live that way; my belief was that *I can recover from this darn old neurogenic bladder.* I had no idea how to do it, but had faith and belief that I would recover.

A few days after the dire report from my urologist, I was sitting in my office when one of our territory managers called. He was in the Duke University Hospital where he had been admitted for extensive biofeedback training. Ike had dangerously high blood pressure and none of the pharmaceutical drugs worked on him; biofeedback was a last resort to get his serious health situation under control.

As fate would have it, a few days later I read an article in *Reader's Digest* about the amazing things being done with biofeedback. My intuition said, "Do it" so I read as much as I could find on biofeedback. According to the NIH website, "Biofeedback is a mind–body technique in which individuals learn how to modify their physiology for the purpose of improving physical, mental, emotional and spiritual health."[140] Although the foundation of biofeedback is based on ancient practices such as meditation, the word was first coined in 1969 and defined as "a real-time physiological mirror."

Although I could find nothing about biofeedback related to a neurogenic bladder, I assumed that if Ike could regulate a body process as complicated as blood pressure, surely I could figure out how to "turn on" my defunct bladder. I created my own visualization of a dark whirlpool emptying by way of a funnel at the bottom of the pool. By meditating on this visualization prior to practicing it, and then affirming my belief that I would recover, after several months my bladder started to function – very poorly, but enough to keep me on track. If I was looking at a life-time of IC, a few months was only a blip in time. It took a full year, but I fully recovered! I didn't realize it at the time, but I had been living what I am now talking about in this book:

- ✓ Belief I would recover
- ✓ Meditation to reinforce my belief
- ✓ Creative visualization to facilitate healing
- ✓ Intuition that it was the right road to recovery

GUIDEPOST

Belief in oneself is required for healing.

-Caroline Myss, PhD

CASE STUDY

She'll never draw again

My mom was a medical and scientific illustrator for the CDC in Atlanta and she did work that went all over the world to enable doctors and scientists to make diagnoses of organisms that invade the human body. She was considered an expert on parasitology and much of her work was in that field.

When she was in her early sixties and still working at CDC she had a bad fall in her home while taking a box fan out of the attic. Mom fell backwards, all the way down the steps, and the fan hit her squarely on her right arm, inches below the shoulder. At the hospital, our family doctor, who was also a close friend, said, "She'll never draw again. There are at least nine fractures and the ulnar nerve is pretty much obliterated."

"Well, don't tell her that!" I said. "If she can never draw again, you might as well take a .45 to her head and put her out of her misery. It will kill her."

The next two months my twin sister and I monitored every phone call and every visitor – and there were plenty. We gave everyone firm instructions: *Tell her she'll be well in no time. DO NOT tell her how serious this injury is.*

In ten weeks, my mom returned to her drawing board in the audio-visual department at CDC and, as her colleagues told me, she went on to do some of the best work in her career. How did mom recover from an injury that could have been life-altering? She believed she would be well.

Because of my mom's experience with her arm, and mine with my bladder, it galls me when someone says their doctor has given them a dire diagnosis and "that's that." My friend, Robert Nash, MD, refers to such proclamations as "words that maim."[141] Why do people relinquish their personal power and beliefs? Why do we think it's okay to reinforce that dire diagnosis because "we don't want to give someone false hope?" When someone we love is facing a serious health challenge, why would we rob them of their belief – the one thing that might facilitate a recovery?

I realize my viewpoint raises a number of ethical questions and moral issues, but that's not my field, so I am leaving this discussion for your consideration. If you doubt my mom's contributions to health and science, Google *Margery Borom CDC* or *Margery R. Borom* CDC to see some of her work.

In our own journey back to wellness, sometimes we have to enlarge our paradigms to make room for new beliefs – and sometimes we have to abandon beliefs that no longer serve us. That's exactly what I had to do when I had crippling back problems and traditional medicine offered me nothing but toxic pharmaceutical drugs. Dr. Kyle Fogel opened an entire new world of healing to me through chiropractic. Had I stuck to my old beliefs, I would probably be in a wheelchair — and addicted to opioids.

To summarize in simple words our talk about belief, I would like to quote the great guru and author, Dr. Wayne Dyer:

You'll see it when you believe it.[142]

SUMMARY

Your Journey along the Mending Map

Hopefully the guideposts on this Mending Map have given you some suggestions that will help you on your own personal journey back to health from illness or injury; however before we adjourn, there is one more guidepost I want to share with you that brings together many of the ideas and concepts we've been talking about:

Mother Nature

You don't have to be a scientist or researcher to recognize the great benefits of nature – just watch children at play in the outdoors to witness their unbound joy and happiness. Even a hospital room with a view of trees has proven to be beneficial because abdominal surgery patients have fewer complications, require less medication for pain, and leave the hospital sooner than those "whose rooms faced a brick wall."[143]

Emerging research is proving to us that there are numerous benefits we can each derive from Mother Nature:

Lowers blood pressure

According to a study in June 2016, almost ten percent of high blood pressure patients who spent only thirty minutes in a park each week were able to lower their hypertension. Since we spend more than $48 billion a year to treat high blood pressure, green space visitations could be "a simple and affordable way to improve heart health."[144]

Lowers cortisol

In the 1980s, the Forest Agency of Japan recommended strolls in the woods to improve health, and research since then has proven the efficacy of this advice. "Spending time in the forest induces a state of physiologic relaxation" according to forest-therapy expert and researcher Yoshifumi Miyazaki of Chiba University in Japan.[145] Dr. Miyazaki found that just 40 minutes of walking in a cedar forest lowered the stress hormone cortisol.

Promotes Cancer-Fighting Cells

Women who live in high vegetation areas have a twelve percent lower risk of death from all cancers when compared to those who live in spaces with less greenery according to a study published in 2016 by *Environmental Health Perspectives*.[146] Dr. Qing Li, a professor at the Nippon Medical School in Tokyo, explains that aromatic compounds (phytoncides) are emitted by plants and trees and, "when inhaled, can spur healthy biological changes in a manner similar to aromatherapy."[147]

When people either walk through the woods, or better yet spend the night in forests, they "often exhibit changes in blood associated with protection against cancer, better immunity, and lower blood pressure."[148] Phytoncides increase the quantity of natural killer (NK) cells, which are a type of white blood cell that is associated with lower cancer risk since it supports the immune system.

Improves depression and anxiety
Ninety minutes of walking in a natural setting can help with depression and anxiety because people who do this are "less likely to ruminate – a hallmark of depression and anxiety" and they also have less brain activity in the area associated with depression.[149] Although the exact way this happens is not yet clear, one of the hypotheses was published in *Frontier in Psychology*[150] - there are high levels of negative ions in the air around mountains, forests, and moving water, and it is believed that these ions have the potential to reduce symptoms of depression. Why would you take a drug when a walk in the woods would give you the same benefit without the side effects?

GUIDEPOST

There is something infinitely healing in the repeated refrains of nature – the assurance that dawn comes after night, and spring after winter.
-Rachel Carson

Calms your mind and spirit

Feelings of awe can cause us to feel more generous and helpful while also lowering the levels of inflammatory agents – but this only happens when we gaze at rolling landscapes or spectacular waterfalls, not skyscrapers.[151] On Goodnet.org, Allison Michelle Dienstman gives us this lovely description of our rewards for being in nature:[152]

> *A long walk in a park on your own gives a chance to clear the mind and can even count as a type of meditation. Spending time in nature helps us live in the moment as we breathe in the air, listen to the sound of the birds chirping, or feel the grass on our feet. Nature can even teach valuable lessons and reveal metaphors to help us connect with our spirituality. The changes of season reflect the peaks and valleys we go through in life. Meanwhile, a coursing river reminds us of our need to "go with the flow" and navigate the waters of life, so to speak.*

I hope you can see the full-spectrum of benefits provided to us by Mother Nature, as well as the Guideposts we have talked about in this book, and how we can use them on our own personal journeys to wellness. Remember, regardless of the cause of your illness or injury, healing must come from within:

Your body and what you feed it,
Your mind and what you think,
Your soul and what you believe.

ACKNOWLEDGEMENTS

With deepest appreciation to the medical professionals who guided me on my own mending map:

    Michael Ciepiela, MD - Orthopaedic Surgeon
    James Wood, MD – Neurosurgeon
    Kamal Kabakibou, MD - Pain Management
    Kyle Fogel, DC - Chiropractor
    Paul Schenk, Psy.D – Psychologist
    Robert A. Nash, MD – Neurologist, Acupuncturist
    Pamela Watson, APRN – Nurse Practitioner
    Kevin Brown, MD – Endocrinologist
    Thomas Demarini, MD – Pulmonologist
    Stephen Salmieri, DO – Gynecological Oncology
    Jimmy Jiang, MD – Orthopaedic Surgeon
    Terry Trundle, PTA, ATC, LAT – Physical Therapist
    Judy Rossi, PT, DPT – Physical Therapist
    Janiece Andrews, MD – Mentor and Friend
    Martha Elizabeth Childs, Pharm.D – Pharmacist

APPENDIX A

Foods can Harm, Foods can Heal

Foods are a grand combination of nature's chemicals that provide our bodies with both the macro and the micro nutrients we need to thrive. Unfortunately, many of our food products been altered by manufacturing processes as well as farming methods, and may have added chemicals with potential harmful side effects. In addition, the naturally occurring chemicals in food can also harm certain physical conditions; but, likewise, many foods can heal us, too.

Here are some of the more common ailments and their interactions with certain foods that either *harm or heal.*

Arthritis: There is some evidence that red meats and fatty foods make inflammation from arthritis worse, so cut down on these foods and eat more fatty fish, such as sardines, salmon, high flavonoid citrus fruits (see Appendix C). Be careful about taking omega-3 supplements. Arthritis drugs can interfere with blood clotting and excessive amounts can increase bleeding risks.

Other beneficial foods for people with arthritis include fresh yellow and green vegetables (high in beta carotene, Vit. C, and antioxidants to lessen cell damage), legumes, peas, oysters, and wheat germ, which have zinc (for immune function), and ginger, which has anti-inflammatory properties.

Asthma: Attacks may be triggered by dairy products, cheese, soy sauce, mushrooms, and yeast breads. Avoid all foods with sulfites. Broth, chicken soup, and other healthy fluids can help thin mucus that forms in the bronchial tubes. Eat plenty of foods to promote a good immune system, such as fresh fruits and vegetables, lean meats, oysters, and yogurt.

Burns: To heal damaged skin and tissues and promote healing, burn patients need high protein foods and zinc and plenty of non-alcoholic drinks to replace fluids; they should avoid tea and coffee, too. To promote healthy skin and fight infection, they should also eat plenty of Vit. C rich foods.

Cancer: The National Cancer Institute estimates that "one-third of all cancers are related to diet."[153] Cancer patients should avoid any food that could have pesticides and/or environmental pollutants[154] and consume wholesome foods and plenty of dark green and yellow vegetables, citrus and other fruits, and whole-grain cereals and breads and high-fiber foods for good colon function. Due to the complicated situations of cancer patients, their diet, and any supplements should be taken under the supervision of a registered dietitian or nutritionist.

Diabetes: This is a complicated disease and your nutrition should be done under the supervision of your doctor and/or nutritionist. Generally, however, diabetics who are insulin dependent should eat regular meals and snacks to maintain consistent blood sugar levels, with a proper balance of complex carbohydrates, proteins, and fat, and high-fiber foods. Be aware that bran cereals may affect absorption of zinc, iron, and other minerals.[155]

Eczema: Foods high in Vitamin B-6 can be helpful to people with eczema, which tends to run in families. B-6 foods include brown rice, wheat germ and legumes. Babies and small children may have eczema (atopic dermatitis) which needs medical supervision.

Gout: Purines are a molecule of carbon and nitrogen atoms and are the building block[156] of all animals and plants. They are so essential to life that the body manufactures them (they are *endogenous*). Purines in foods we eat are *exogenous* (they come from outside the body). It is these exogenous purines that can cause problems because when we eat them, the byproduct of our metabolism is *uric acid.*

In some people, too much uric acid in the blood (hyperuricemia) causes the formation of kidney stones or inflammation in joints (gout).

High purine foods include organ (i.e., liver) and game meats (venison) seafood, high fructose corn syrup, supplements with yeast or yeast extract, and saturated fats. Foods that have moderate amounts of purines include these vegetables: mushrooms, asparagus, spinach, green peas, and cauliflower.

Stroke: People who consume 4,300 mg a day of potassium are almost 40% less likely to have a stroke than those who only eat the 2,500 in the average American diet.[157] Good sources of potassium include sweet potato, chicken, turkey and other lean meats, low-fat cheese, leafy greens such as cooked spinach, bananas, and whole-grain bread.

Consumption of too much potassium can be dangerous for some people, such as those with kidney disorders[158] so never take potassium supplements without talking to your medical professional first.

For an excellent resource on *Foods that Harm, Foods that Heal,* I refer you to the *Reader's Digest* publication:

https://www.amazon.com/Foods-That-Harm-Heal/dp/0762106050

APPENDIX B

Herb, Drug and Supplement Interactions

Although we don't have much information on the interactions of supplements and herbs with pharmaceutical drugs, we do know that there are potentially many harmful reactions, so please be cautious. Some interactions may increase a drug's effects, so that you get too much, and others may lead to diminished effectiveness, so you don't get the benefit of the drug.

You may be on a drug with a *narrow therapeutic range*[159] that is absolutely essential to your health and well-being. This is a class of drugs that must be maintained at an extremely specific level, and either too little or too much can cause big problems and includes drugs for:

- Preventing organ transplant rejections (Cyclosporine)
- Anti-coagulant (Warfarin)
- Heart problems (Digoxin)
- Thyroid problems (Levothyroxine)

To be safe, take your bottles of herbs and supplements to your medical appointments so your physician will have the correct information for counseling you on this very important topic. Here is a partial list of some **common herb-drug interactions:**

Black Cohosh – taken for symptoms of menopause and hot flashes, can reduce the efficacy of cisplatin (a cancer drug) and may increase the chance of side effects with antibiotics, antidepressants, antihypertensives (beta-blockers, calcium-channel blockers), statins, and Tylenol

CBD Oil – though touted as a miracle healer, research is sketchy and inconclusive[160]. We do know that it blocks certain enzymes that are needed to metabolize some drugs such as anti-depressants, statins, and calcium channel blockers. Don't take CDB oil until you talk to your doctor and/or pharmacist.

Echinacea – believed to treat infections and improve the immune system; has potentially serious side effects when taken with Allegra, Halcion, Dilantin, Theo-Dur, Coumadin, statins, Orinase.[161]

Garlic – touts a number of benefits but may reduce drug efficacy of antihypertensives, HIV protease inhibitors, immunosuppressants, and oral contraceptives; potential for dangerous increase in drug efficacy for blood thinners and drugs for diabetes.[162]

Ginkgo Biloba – treats impotence and may improve mental processes; can reduce efficacy of certain diuretics and cause dangerous rise in efficacy of antidepressants and blood thinners.

Ginseng – has anti-inflammatory and antioxidant properties but may cause dangerous rise in drug efficacy of blood thinners and drugs for diabetes.[163]

Green Tea – has natural antioxidants; increased risk of side effects with Tegretol, Aldomet, Cordarone, Tylenol; reduced efficacy of diabetes drugs and dangerous increase in efficacy of blood thinners.

Saw Palmetto – known for benefits to men; reduces efficacy of Estrace, Premarin, and oral contraceptive; potential for dangerous rise in efficacy of blood thinners, prostate, and hair-growth drugs.

St. John's Wort – this herb can be an effective treatment for depression but can decrease the effectiveness of birth control pills and other pharmaceuticals; it has many potentially harmful side effects when taken with drugs; here is a full list: https://www.nccih.nih.gov/health/know-science/how-medications-supplements-interact/page-5.[164]

Food and pharmaceutical drugs taken by mouth all end up in your digestive tract and since they are all chemicals, they interact with one another – and sometimes the resulting reaction is not good, and can even be dangerous.[165] For example, MAO inhibitors used to treat depression (and blood pressure in some people) should never be mixed with the amino acid tyramine, which is found in bologna, chicken liver, processed meats, legumes, soy sauce, beer and some red wines. Within minutes of mixing this drug with any of these foods, symptoms will develop and may even lead to death.[166]

      Fortunately, drug manufacturers are required to put notices of such potential side effects in their product flyers attached to prescriptions – but how many people take the time to read them? It's in your best interest to do so.

Taking drugs with or without food is also critical to the drug's effectiveness, and this, too, is in those flyers. Do yourself a favor and always read those inserts. There are too many possibilities for drug and food interactions to include here, but this list will give you some common ones.

DRUG	FOOD INTERACTION / PROBLEM
Antiarrhythmics	Avoid caffeine; irregular heartbeat
Codeine	Constipation
Aspirin, NSAIDS	Always take with food; lowers Vit. C and folate absorption
Steroids	Fluid retention increases with salty foods; causes deficiency of calcium, potassium, Vit. K
Antacids	Interfere with absorption of certain minerals, such as calcium
Digitalis	Increases loss of potassium; avoid milk and high fiber foods which reduce absorption
Dilantin, phenobarbital	Deficiency of folate, B vitamins; increases risk of anemia and nerve problems
Sulfa drugs	Risk of Vit. B_{12} deficiency
Tetracycline	Lowers Vit. C absorption; efficacy reduced by dairy products
Theophylline	Drug toxicity risk with consumption of caffeine; charbroiled and high-protein foods reduce absorption
Pseudoephedrine	Caffeine increases anxiety, nervousness
Alpha blockers	Excessive drop in blood pressure if not taken with food or beverage (non-alcohol)

Vitamin/Mineral and drug interactions can also cause complications and lead to poor outcomes[167] and risk factors can increase for those who take multiple drugs, are older, or who have liver and kidney problems. This list provides a few of the potential problems with vitamins, minerals, and drugs; you should to talk to your health-care professional if you use supplements.[168]

VITAMIN	DRUG / PROBLEM or BENEFIT
A	Retinoids – nausea, vomiting, blurred vision, poor muscle coordination
B_6	Decreases efficacy of levodopa and phenytoin
E	Warfarin – increased bleeding risk; can also interfere with anesthetics
K	Warfarin – DVT, embolism, myocardial infarction, stroke
Niacin	Statins – muscle weakness or breakdown; renal failure
Folic Acid	Used as prophylaxis to prevent toxicities from Methotrexate
Calcium	Numerous interactions – talk to doctor and/or pharmacist
Magnesium	Can lower efficacy of certain antibiotics
Iron	Can interfere with absorption of certain antibiotics, levodopa
Potassium	Numerous interactions – talk to doctor and/or pharmacist

Pharmaceutical drugs, vitamins, minerals, and herbs can all play a role in our health – but many times these players should not be on the same team. For additional information on drug, herb, and supplement interactions, please see the website of the National Center for Complementary and Integrative Medicine, which is part of the National Institutes of Health:

https://www.nccih.nih.gov/health/know-science/how-medications-supplements-interact?

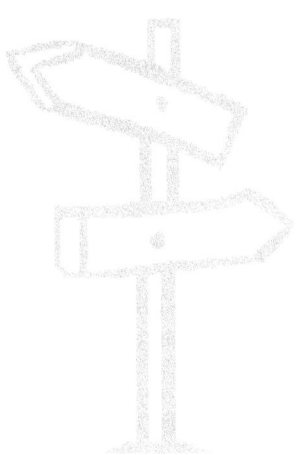

APPENDIX C

Plant Chemicals that Protect Us

Just like humans and other animals, plants, too, are susceptible to various viruses and cancer. To protect themselves, they have phytochemicals (from the Greek word for plant – *phyton*) and emerging research indicates that these *phytochemicals* can also protect us.

PHYTOCHEMICAL	SOURCE	USE
Allylic sulfide	Onions, garlic	Stimulates protective enzymes
Bioflavonoids	Most fresh fruits, veggies	Antioxidants; inhibit hormones that promote cancer
Catechins / tannins	Berries, green tea	Antioxidant
Curcumin	Turmeric, cumin	Tobacco carcinogen protection
Genistein	Broccoli, cabbage, kale, other cruciferous	Tumor growth inhibiting
Indoles	Broccoli, cabbage, cauliflower, mustard greens	Inhibit estrogen that may stimulate some cancers; makes protective enzymes
Isoflavones	Beans, peanuts, peas, other legumes	Destroy cancer enzymes; slow uptake of estrogen
Isothiocyanates	Mustard, radishes, and horseradish	Protective enzyme production
Lignans	Flaxseed, walnuts, fatty fish	Block prostaglandins, inhibit estrogen

PHYTOCHEMICAL	SOURCE	USE
Limonoids	Citrus fruits	Protective enzymes
Lycopene	Tomatoes, watermelon, pink grapefruit	Antioxidants; prostate cancer protection
Monoterepenes	Citrus fruits, broccoli, basil, orange & yellow veggies	Antioxidant; aid protective enzyme activity
Omega-3 Fatty Acids	Flaxseeds, canola oil, fatty fish, walnuts	Reduce inflammation and inhibit estrogen
Phenolic Acid	Whole grains, egg-plant, carrots, citrus, peppers, parsley, tomatoes, teas, berries, broccoli, cabbage	Inhibit nitrosamines and improve enzyme activity (nitrosamines are chemicals used in manufacturing that are generally carcinogenic)
Protease	Soybeans	Destroy the enzyme inhibitors that help spread cancer
Quercetin	Red & white wines; grape skins	Inhibit inflammation, clots, mutation of cells
Terpenes	Citrus fruits	Energize anticancer enzymes

INDEX

5-HTP, 43
Abigail Brenner, M.D, 114
Aces, 36
acid, 52, 53, 55, 56
Acupuncture, 60, 190
Adrenalin, 130
affirmation, 102, 109, 110
alcohol, 42, 50, 176
alkaline, 55
allergies, 60
Allison Michelle Dienstman, 166
allopathy, 60
almonds, 51, 53, 54
alternative therapies, 59, 67
Alzheimer, 52
Alzheimer's, 52
American, 51, 56
American College of Surgeons, 12
American Physical Therapy Association, 72
amino acid, 34, 43, 175
amino acids, 34, 52
anabolism, 30
anemia, 52, 54
Antibiotics, 37
antibodies, 34, 51
anti-inflammatory, 22, 23, 32, 65, 71, 169, 174
anti-oxidant, 53, 57
Antioxidants, 36, 179, 180
anxiety, 39, 63, 111, 112, 126, 135, 165, 176
arnica, 98, 99
Arnica, 98
Aromatherapy, 63
arteries, 53
arthritis, 51, 60, 63
Ascorbic Acid, 53
asthma, 24, 25, 26, 55, 148

At First Sight, i, 100
B-12, 52
B-2, 51
Bananas, 57
B-complex, 52, 53
beans, 51, 53, 54, 56
belief, 2, 139, 143, 157, 158, 159, 160, 161, 162
beliefs, 114, 131, 132, 135, 155, 158, 161, 162
Bengals, 152
bile, 53
Biofeedback, 63
Bioflavonoids, 53
Biotin, 52
blood, 49, 51, 52, 53, 54, 56, 64
blood pressure, 51
Board certified, 12
Bob Proctor, 90
bones, 54, 55, 56
brain, 52, 54, 56, 57
brainwaves, 42
Breathe, 86, 93, 101, 102, 105
breathing, 24, 42, 48, 79, 86, 93, 102, 105, 113, 148
brewer's yeast, 51, 52, 53, 57, 58
broccoli, 51, 52, 53
brown rice, 34, 51, 52, 171
Bruce Lipton, PhD, 134
buckwheat, *52, 53*
burn, ii, 121, 170
burns, *53, 63*
C complex, *53*
CDC, 24
caffeine, 42, *60*, 176
calcium, 54, 55
Calcium, 55, 177
cancer, 50, 54
Cancer-Fighting Cells, 164

CAPP, 72
carbohydrates, 48, 51
cardiologist, 1, 2
Carolyn Myss, PhD, 147
carrots, 51
catabolism, 30
cauliflower, 53
cancer, ii, 6, 7, 39, 107, 108, 157, 170, 174, 179, 180
CDC, 54, 97, 160, 161, 162
cell, 52, 56
cells, 49, 52, 57
cellular, 54
cereals, 56, 57
Cherries, 45
children, i, 13, 14, 51, 55, 56, 91, 127, 147, 148, 171
Chiropractors, 60
cholesterol, 51, 53
Choline, 52
Chromium, 56
chromium picolinate, 56
chromium polynicotinate, 56
citrus fruit skins, 53
Co-Enzyme Q-10, 48
colds, 53
collagen, 53
colon, 54, 63
Columbia University, 72
Common Sense Medicine, i, iii
complementary, 59, 63, 67
connective tissue, 64
conscious, 100, 105, 114, 146
constipation, 37, 38, 39
copper, 55, 56, 58
Copper, 56
Co-Q-10, 48, 49
cortisol, 97, 164
Cortisol, 130
Cousins, 126
Cyano Cobalamin, 52

deep sleep, 42
depression, 52, 87, 115, 142, 165, 175
Descartes, 140
diagnosis, 4, 7, 11, 26, 61, 147, 156, 157, 161
digestion, 48, 51
disease, 50, 60, 61, 62
diseases, 50
diuretics, 57
DNA, 52
do no harm, 19, 22
doctor's credentials, 62
Dr. Ciepiela, 152
Dr. Dean Ornish, 108
Dr. Eman Elkadry, 71
Dr. Fogel, 66
Dr. Hye-Chun Hur, 72
Dr. Keiko Hayashi, 126
Dr. Larry Dossey, 139
Dr. Larry Strasburger, 120
Dr. Mark Hymen, 104
Dr. Mehl-Madrona, 156
Dr. Michael E. McCullough, 87
Dr. Peter Mitchell, 48
Dr. Qing Li, 164
Dr. Robert A. Emmons, 87
Dr. Schenk, 115, 116
Dr. Strasburger, 120
Dr. Wayne Dyer, 90, 162
drowsy, 43
Drug Interactions, 78
druggist, 20, 22, 24, 55
drugs, 20, 21, 23, 24, 25, 26, 35, 37, 43, 47, 49, 55, 62, 65, 78, 79, 80, 97, 98, 99, 100, 125, 132, 159, 162, 169, 173, 174, 175, 176, 177, 178, 190
Dyer, 63, 90, 92, 135

EFT, i, 63, 129, 132, 133, 134, 135
Elderly, 50
Emory University Hospital, 6
Emotional Freedom Technique, 63
Endorphins, 98, 125
energy, 49, 51, 60, 64, 65
Energy Psychology, 63
enzymes, 48, 49, 55
Enzymes, 49
Ernest Rosenbaum, MD, 7
errors in judgment, 19
essential minerals, 55
essential nutrients, 33
exercise, 31, 42, 69, 102, 143
Exercise, 56
eyes, 51
family and friends, 18, 105, 121
Fasting, 63
fasting program, 64
fat, 31, 32, 35, 47, 48, 50, 170, 171
fats, 57
fatty acids, 32, 35, 36
finances, 15, 90
five senses, 145
Florence Scovel, 150
Folic Acid, 52, 177
food, 48, 49, 50, 53, 55
Framingham Heart Study, 55
free radicals, 53, 54, 57
Fresh foods, 57
frontal lobe, 111
fruits, 53, 63
fuel, 48
garlic, 57
glands, 51
glucose, 56
good bacteria, 37, 38

grapefruit, 52
Gratitude Questionnaire, 88
green peppers, 53
greens, 53
growth, 51, 56
hair, 57, 58, 64
Hair Analysis, 64
Harvard, 71, 72, 132, 147, 190
Healing the Mind through the Power of Story, 155
health care, 61
health practitioners, 61
health professional, i, 57, 58, 64
heart, 55
heart patients, 48
hemoglobin, 56, 65
herbs, 47, 78, 99, 143, 173, 178
high blood pressure, 159, 164
Hippocratic Oath, 19
HMO, 2
Holistic, 60
homeopathy, 60, 61
Homeopathy, 60, 61, 190
Honey, 43, 44
house, 14, 15, 16, 17, 55, 156
hypertension, 55, 60, 63
hypnosis, 64
Hypnosis, 64
ICU, 16
immune, 51, 52, 53, 54, 57, 61
immune system, 51, 53, 54, 57, 61
immunity, 34, 112
Inositol, 53
insomnia, 51, 60
Interoception, 145
intestinal, 54
intuition, 145, 146, 147, 148, 149, 150, 159
Intuition, ii, 145, 146, 150, 160
Iodine, 57

Iridologists, 61
iron, 55, 56
Iron, 56, 177
James Wood, MD, 167
Janiece Andrews, MD, 167
Jed Foundation, 83
Jennifer Williamson, 109
Jimmy Jiang, MD, 167
Johns Hopkins, 7
Joseph Campbell, 154
Josh Clark, 143
Judith Orloff, MD, 147
Judy Rossi, PT, DPT, 167
Kamal Kabakibou, MD, 167
Kevin Brown, MD, 167
kidneys, 63
Kinesiology, 61
kiwi, 53
knee, 8, 31, 69, 128
Kyle Fogel, DC, 167
laughter, ii, 126, 127, 128
Lavender, 39
legumes, 51, 52, 56, 57
Lissa Rankin, MD, 135
low energy, 48
L-tryptophan, 43
lungs, 63
macro-nutrients, 47
magnesium, 55
Magnesium, 44, 55, 177
malnutrition, 32, 33
Malted Milk, 43
Manganese, 57
Margery Borom, 162
Martha Elizabeth Childs, Pharm.D, 167
Mary Kay Ashe, 110
Massage Therapy, 64
Maya Angelou, 92
Mayo Clinic, 85, 88
meals, 13, 17, 22, 90, 170

medical team, 12
medical tests, ii
medications, 9, 14, 17, 20, 22, 33, 43, 48, *50*, 175, 178
medicine, *61*
memory molecule, *54*
metabolism, 52, 55, 56, 57
MGM, i, 100
Miami School of Medicine, 7
Michael Ciepiela, MD, 167
micro-nutrients, 47, 49
mineral, 55, 56, 57, 60
minerals, 49, 55, 58, 64
Minerals, 55, 56
Miss USA, 146
molasses, 53
Mona Lisa Schulz, MD, 147
Mother Nature, 95, 163
MS, 156, 157, 158
multiple sclerosis, 156
muscle, 52, 54, 55, 60, 63
muscles, 55, 64
Mushrooms, 58
myofascial pain, 71
national averages, 12
National Institutes of Health, 87, 147, 178
National Library of Medicine, 139
natural, 54, 61
natural therapies, 61
Naturopaths, 61
nerve, 51, 54, 55, 57, 60
nervous system, 51, 52, 56
neuroma, 8
neurotransmitter, 52
Newtonian physics, 140
Niacin, 51
NIH, 87, 147, 159
Nippon Medical School, 164
Nobel Prize, 48

Norman Cousins, 126
Norman Shealy, MD, 147
Nova Care, 10
nutrients, 55
nutrition, 61
nutritionals, 17
nuts, 27, 30, 32, 34, 36, 39, 51, 52, 56, 57
oats, 53
Oilers, 152
omega-3, 169
omega-6, 35
onions, 53
oranges, 53
Oregano, 39
organs, 60, 65
orthopedists, 62
osteopaths, 62
Osteopathy, 62
oxygen, 55, 56
P.A., 4, 10, 11
P.A.s, 9
P.T., 20, 21
pain, i, 22, 27, 28, 41, 60, 63, 64, 65, 66, 69, 71, 72, 75, 85, 91, 93, 95, 96, 97, 98, 99, 100, 101, 102, 104, 105, 111, 112, 114, 115, 116, 119, 126, 130, 132, 142, 152, 163
pain control, 63
Pamela Watson, APRN, 167
Pantothenic Acid, 51
papaya, 53
Para-Aminobenzoic Acid, 53
parietal lobe, 111
pasta, 34
PDR, 79
peanut butter, 53
peas, 53, 54
pelvic floor, 71, 72
pelvic floor therapy, 71, 72
Peppermint, 39

pets, 14
pH, 55
Phenergan, 79
phosphorus, 54, 55, 56
Phosphorus, 56
Physical Therapist, 10, 20, 22, 70
physical therapy, 10, 20, 31, 42, 65, 69, 70, 72, 73, 75, 89, 90, 121
Physician's Assistants, 9
phytoncides, 164
Phytoncides, 165
pineapple, *57*
plateaus, i, 70, 89, 90
Plateaus, 70
Play it Safe, 76
potassium, 55, 57
Potassium, 57
potatoes, 53, 54
PPO, 2
prayer, 139, 141, 142, 143, 157
Proctor, 92
Proprioception, 145
protein, 32, 34, 39, *56*, 170, 176
proteins, 48, 49, 56
Proteins, 33, 34
psychology, 130, 131
Psychology Today, 83, 146, 153, 190
Psychoneuroimmunology, 127
PTSD, i, 121, 122, 129, 130
pulmonologist, 24, 55
purines, 30, 171
Pyridoxine, 52
Rapid Eye Movement, 42
RDA, 50, 57
Reader's Digest, 159, 172
Recommended Dietary Allowances, 50

recovery, 2, 12, 22, 41, 45, 71, 73, 75, 84, 89, 90, 92, 93, 110, 121, 129, 148, 152, 157, 160, 161
recuperation, 37, 122
references, 62
referral, 3, 8
Reflexology, *65*
Reinventing Medicine, 139
relaxation, *63, 64*
REM, 42
REM sleep, 42
reticular formation, 111
Riboflavin, 51
Ribonucleic Acid, 54
Robert A. Nash, M.D, iii
Robert C. Coghill, PhD, 96
Robert Nash, MD, 161
Rosemary, 39
Sage, 39
Saints, 152
scopolamine, 79
Scott D. Allison, PhD, 153
Sea kelp, 57
Second opinions, 7
Second Opinions, 5, 8
seeds, 34, 36, 51
seeing, 48
selenium, 54, 55
Selenium, 57
serotonin, 41, 43, 44, 60
sesame seeds, 57
skin, 51, 52, 54, 57, 58, 63
sleep, 41, 42, 43, 44, 45, 60, 64, 87, 105, 112, 126, 190
sodium, 57
spicy foods, 42
Stanford University School of Medicine, 7, 155
Star Wars, 154
statins, 48

stress, i, 6, 13, 15, 18, 50, 51, 60, 61, 76, 83, 95, 97, 98, 102, 104, 105, 108, 129, 164
subconscious, 114, 132
Sue Johnson, Clinical Psychologist, 135
sugar, 57
sun, 53
supplements, 17, 20, 32, 33, 34, 47, 49, *53, 57, 58,* 78, 169, 170, 171, 172, 173, 175, 177, 178
sweat, 50
tasting, 48
TBS, 10
teeth, 54, 55, 56
TENS unit, 98
Terri Britt, 146
Terry Trundle, PTA, ATC, LAT, 167
thalamus, 111
The New England Journal of Medicine, 127
Therapeutic Touch, 65
Thiamine, 51
thinking, 48
Thomas Demarini, MD, 167
Thomas Jefferson, 153
thoughts, 63, 83, 84, 85, 86, 89, 91, 92, 93, 94, 97, 102, 107, 108, 109, 110, 112, 113, 127, 131, 141
Thyme, 39
thyroid, 57
Tocopherol, 54
tomatoes, 52, 53, 54
Tony Robbins, 63
toxic, 50, 51, 56, 63, 64
trace minerals, 55
United States, 60
University of Tsukuba, 126

urologists, 62
vegetable, 52
vegetables, 51, 53, 54, 55, 57
Vestibular, 145
veterinarians, 61
viruses, 53
vitamin, 50, 51, 52, 53, 60
Vitamin A, 51, 54
Vitamin B-1, 51
Vitamin B-5, 51
Vitamin B-6, 52
Vitamin C, 53
Vitamin D, 54
Vitamin E, 54
vitamins, 49, 50, 55, 57
Wake Forest University
   School of Medicine, 95
warfarin, 99
warm bath, 43
Warm Milk, 43
water, 50
WCS, 72
wheat germ, 51, 53, 54, 57, 58
whole grain breads, 34
whole grains, 51, 52, 56, 57
William James, 99
x-rays, 62
yeast, 52, 54, 56
zinc, 55, 58
Zinc, 57
zucchini, 53

ENDNOTES

[1] *Help yourself to Seconds*. AARP Bulletin, page 18, February 2003
[2] Ibid.
[3] Ibid.
[4] Ibid.
[5] Ibid.
[6] https://health.gov/hcq/ade.asp
[7] Naturalnews.com/046371_digestime_herb_peppermint_natural_medicinel.html
[8] Ibid
[9] Southern Community Cohort Study Newsletter, Issue 13, 2014, referencing the Health Professionals Follow-up Study (based on data from 76,000 women and 42,000 men).
[10] http://www.caring.com/articles/five-foods-that-help-you-sleep?
[11] http://www.rd.com/health/beauty/foods-that-help-you-sleep/
[12] *Psychology Today*, Dale Archer, M.D., *Vitamin D Deficiency and Depression*, www.Psychologytoday.com, Jul 11, 2013
[13] Hardie, Ann, *Prescribed drugs make one in four elderly people ill*" The Atlanta Constitution, July 27, 1994. p. 1.
[14] Neag, Ray, "Catheter Helps Prevent Sepsis in Bloodstream," *The Wall Street Journal,* September 27, 1994.
[15] Pomeranz B: Recent advances in Acupuncture Research, *Temple Univ. Center for Frontier Sciences Symposium,* April 26, 1994.
[16] FitzGerald, Frances E., "Understanding Homeopathy," *Health Counselor*, Vol. 5, No. 2, pp. 23, 24.
[17] FitzGerald, p. 24.
[18] Dracker, Pune, "Heal Spot, Heal." *ASPCA Animal Watch*, Fall 1994, p. 20.
[19] *Harvard Women's Health Watch*, June 2018
https://www.health.harvard.edu/womens-health/pelvic-physical-therapy-another-potential-treatment-option
[20] Ibid
[21] Ibid
[22] Ibid
[23] https://columbiasurgery.org/colorectal/pelvic-floor-disorders-frequently-asked-questions

[24] *Harvard Women's Health Watch,* June 2018 https://www.health.harvard.edu/womens-health/pelvic-physical-therapy-another-potential-treatment-option
[25] Well Aware, Summer 2001, published by BCBS of Georgia.
[26] Ron Breazeale, PhD, *Thoughts, Neurotransmitters, Mind-Body Connection,* https://www.psychologytoday.com/us/blog/in-the-face-adversity/201207/thoughts-neurotransmitters-body-mind-connection#:~:text=Neurotransmitters%20control%20virtually%20all%20of,us%20for%20whatever%20is%20expected.z
[27] https://www.jedfoundation.org/positivity/?gclid=EAIaIQobChMI2OmHkuTt6gIVk4zICh0oMwLSEAAYBCAAEgLfS_D_BwE#card=2
[28] www.drpattilevin.com
[29] https://drpattilevin.com/educational-materials/
[30] https://www.mayoclinic.org/healthy-lifestyle/stress-management/in-depth/positive-thinking/art-20043950?pg=2
[31] https://www.positivityblog.com/how-to-stay-positive/
[32] https://www.positivityblog.com/how-to-stay-positive/
[33] https://www.psychologytoday.com/us/blog/what-mentally-strong-people-dont-do/201504/7-scientifically-proven-benefits-gratitude
[34] https://www.webster-dictionary.org/definition/Grateful
[35] https://www.ncbi.nlm.nih.gov/pmc/articles/PMC3010965/
[36] https://sofia.com.sg/wp-content/uploads/2017/11/The-Gratitude-Questionnaire.pdf
[37] https://www.mayoclinic.org/healthy-lifestyle/stress-management/in-depth/positive-thinking/art-20043950?pg=2
[38] https://www.mayoclinic.org/healthy-lifestyle/stress-management/in-depth/positive-thinking/art-20043950?pg=2
[39] https://colinfalconer.org/
[40] https://www.lifehack.org/articles/communication/10-steps-fight-your-way-out-despair-and-find-happiness-again.html
[41] https://tinybuddha.com/author/jan-tucker/
[42] https://tinybuddha.com/blog/7-steps-to-overcome-daily-despair-and-start-living-again/
[43] Prevention, January 2006, www.prevention.com *Think away pain,* pg. 38
[44] Ibid
[45] Ibid

[46] https://www.cdc.gov/mmwr/volumes/66/wr/mm6629a8.htm?s_cid=mm6629a8_w
[47] https://www.healthline.com/health-news/1-in-6-working-in-pain#2
[48] https://www.medicalnewstoday.com/articles/323632
[49] Memorial Sloan Kettering Cancer Center website: https://www.mskcc.org/cancer-care/integrative-medicine/herbs/arnica
[50] Ibid
[51] https://www.psychologytoday.com/us/blog/living-forward/201412/improve-how-you-feel-changing-your-attention and James, W. *The Principles of Psychology, Volume 1.* Holt and Company: New York. 1890.
[52] Jennice Vilhauer, PhD, www.psychologytoday.com, Dec. 6, 2014.
[53] MedLine Plus, U.S. National Library of Medicine, https://medlineplus.gov/ency/article/003211.htm#:~:text=Stress%20is%20a%20feeling%20of,danger%20or%20meet%20a%20deadline.
[54] Anne Sholle, The Center for Mind Body Medicine, July 17, 2015, https://cmbm.org/blog/5-ways-relieve-stress/
[55] Ibid.
[56] Vatche Bartekian, AskMen.com; *The Workaholics Guide to Relaxation*
[57] Bret Stetka, *Changing our DNA through Mind Control?* Scientific American, Dec. 16, 2014. https://www.scientificamerican.com/article/changing-our-dna-through-mind-control/#:~:text=The%20body%20and%20mind%20appear,Linda%20E.
[58] Ibid.
[59] Ibid.
[60] Catharine Paddock, PhD, *Prostate Cancer Genes Altered by Intensive Diet and Lifestyle Changes,* Proceedings of the National Academy of Sciences, June 16, 2008, reported in Medical News Today, June 18, 2008. https://www.medicalnewstoday.com/articles/111710#1
[61] Emily Fletcher *Why Meditation & Visualization Aren't the Same (And How to Use Them)* Sept. 10, 2015, MBG Mindfulness. www.mind-body-green.com

[62] Mind Tools, *Using Affirmations – Harnessing Positive Thinking.* https://www.mindtools.com/pages/article/affirmations.htm#:~:text=What%20Are%20Affirmations%2C%20and%20Do,start%20to%20make%20positive%20changes.
[63] Ibid.
[64] Ibid.
[65] Ibid.
[66] Ibid.
[67] Dr. Carmen Harra, *35 Affirmations that will Change your Life,* Huff Post, Nov. 6, 2018, https://www.huffpost.com/entry/affirmations_b_3527028
[68] Ibid
[69] Jennifer Williamson, *25 Loving Affirmations for Health that respect the Healing Process,* Jan. 29, 2018. https://healingbrave.com/blogs/all/affirmations-for-health-healing-process
[70] Chow, Susan. *Meditation History.* News-Medical. https://www.news-medical.net/health/Meditation-History.aspx. (accessed August 07, 2020)
[71] Cooper, Beth Elle, *What is Meditation and how does affects our Brains.* Aug. 21, 2013. www.Buffer.com
[72] Ibid.
[73] Ibid.
[74] Ibid.
[75] May, Kate Torgovnick post on TEDblog.com, Jan. 11, 2013, *4 Scientific studies on how meditation can affect heart, brain, and creativity.* https://blog.ted.com/4-scientific-studies-on-how-meditation-can-affect-your-heart-brain-and-creativity/
[76] Matthew Thorpe, MD, PhD, Health Line, July 5, 2017. *12 Science-Based Benefits of Meditation.* https://www.healthline.com/nutrition/12-benefits-of-meditation
[77] US National Library of Medicine, Apr. 15, 2009, *The underlying anatomical correlates of long-term meditation: Larger hippocampal and frontal volumes of gray matter"* by Eileen Ludus, Arthur W. Toga, Natasha Lepore, Christian Gaser. https://www.ncbi.nlm.nih.gov/pmc/articles/PMC3184843/
[78] https://mindworks.org/blog/top-tips-on-how-to-meditate/

[79] Abigail Brenner, MD. Psychology Today, *The Benefits of Creative Visualization*, Jun. 25, 2016.
https://www.psychologytoday.com/us/blog/influx/201606/the-benefits-creative-visualization
[80] Ibid.
[81] Ibid.
[82] Ibid.
[83] Ibid.
[84] Rezzan Huseyin, *How Successful People Self-Steward – a Crash Course in Creative Visualization*. http://www.artofwellbein http://www.artofwellbeing.com/2016/03/25/creative-visualization/ g.com/2016/03/25/creative-visualization/
[85] Andrea Blundell. *Why we put the blame on others – and the Real Cost we pay*. HarleyTherapy.co.uk. Sept. 10, 2015
[86] Larry H. Strasburger, MD. *The Litigant-Patient: Mental Health Consequences of Civil Litigation*. J Am Acad Psychiatry Law, Vol. 27, No. 2, 1999, Page 204
[87] Ibid.
[88] Ibid.
[89] T.G. Gutheil, H. Bursztajn, A. Brodsky: A: *Malpractice prevention through the sharing of uncertainty: informed consent and the therapeutics alliance*. N Engl. J. Med 311:49-51, 1984.
[90] Enjuris.com: *Is being a personal injury Plaintiff Stressful?* https://www.enjuris.com/blog/resources/personal-injury-lawsuit-stress/
[91] Andrea Blundell. *Why we put the blame on others – and the Real Cost we pay*. HarleyTherapy.co.uk. Sept. 10, 2015
[92] Ibid.
[93] Hazel Spurr, Aug. 30, 2018, https://medium.com/@hazelspurr/its-official-laughter-lowers-blood-sugar-levels-898ba54ebe85
[94] Hazel Spurr, Aug. 30, 2018, https://medium.com/@hazelspurr/its-official-laughter-lowers-blood-sugar-levels-898ba54ebe85
[95] https://care.diabetesjournals.org/content/26/5/1651.full.
[96] https://en.wikipedia.org/wiki/Norman_Cousins#:~:text=Illness%2C%20laugh%20therapy%20and%20recovery,-Cousins%20did%20research&text=Rusk's%20rehabilitation%20clinic%20confirmed%20this,a%20diagnosis%20of%20ankylosing%20spondylitis.&text=%22I%20made%20the%20joyous%20discovery,free%20sleep%2C%22%20he%20reported.

[97] Folkart, Burt A. (December 1, 1990). "Norman Cousins, 75; Editor, Author, Philosopher, UCLA Teacher". *latimes.com*. Los Angeles Times. Retrieved July 19, 2017.
[98] Barbara Bradley Hagerty. *Laughing back to health*. NPR.org. May 17, 2009.
https://www.npr.org/templates/story/story.php?storyId=104139384
[99] Ibid.
[100] Craig Weiner, DC www.EFTtappingTraining.com
The Art and Science of EFThttps://www.efttappingtraining.com/how-trauma-alters-memory-eft-amygdala-hippocampus/
[101] Lipton, Bruce H. *The Biology of Belief: Unleashing the Power of Consciousness, Matter, and Miracles*. Santa Rosa, CA: Mountain of Love/Elite, 2005. Print.
[102] Downline Dynamics, how to build a happy, health downline, Janiece C Andrews, MD, Jan. 21, 2013, pg. 13.
[103] https://www.thetappingsolution.com/tapping-101/
[104] Larry Dossey, M.D. *Reinventing Medicine – beyond mind-body to a new era of healing*. Harper Collins Publishers, NY 1999, pg. 9
[105] Indian Journal of Psychiatry Oct-Dec 2009. *Prayer and healing: A medical and scientific perspective on randomized controlled trials.*" Ncbi.nlm.gov/pmc/articles/PMC2802370/
[106] Larry Dossey, M.D. *Reinventing Medicine – beyond mind-body to a new era of healing*. Harper Collins Publishers, NY 1999, pg. 21
[107] Linda Wilkins. *Research on Prayer and Healing: Past Present and Future Challenges."* A Thesis submitted to Baylor University. Pg.1. https://baylor-ir.tdl.org/bitstream/handle/2104/9453/FINALThesisDocumentLBW1.pdf;sequence=1
[108] Ibid.
[109] Robert A Nash, MD. *Common Sense Medicine – a Medical Doctor's Prescription for Health Care*. iUniverse, Inc. 2000. Pg. 45
[110] Ibid.
[111] Ibid.
[112] http://www.stangrof.com/
[113] Larry Dossey, M.D. *Reinventing Medicine – beyond mind-body to a new era of healing*. Harper Collins Publishers, NY 1999, pg. 79

[114] WebMD Feature Reviewed by Michael W. Smith, MD on March 26, 2004 https://www.webmd.com/balance/features/can-prayer-heal#5
[115] Ibid.
[116] *7 Proven Health Benefits of Prayer.* https://www.retyrsmart.com/7-proven-health-benefits-of-prayer/
[117] Josh Clark. *Can prayer heal people?* https://health.howstuffworks.com/wellness/natural-medicine/alternative/prayer-healing.htm
[118] The Center for Life Skills. *What is this 8th sense, Interoception:* https://center4lifeskills.com/what-is-this-8th-sense-interoception/
[119] Francis P. Cholle. *What is Intuition and how do we use it?* Psychology Today. Aug. 3, 2011. https://www.psychologytoday.com/us/blog/the-intuitive-compass/201108/what-is-intuition-and-how-do-we-use-it
[120] Terri Britt. *Is being Psychic a Sin?* www.TerriBritt.com
[121] US National Library of Medicine, National Institutes of Health. *Clinical Intuition in Family Medicine: More than first Impressions.* Ann Fam Med. 2013, Jan. https://www.ncbi.nlm.nih.gov/pmc/articles/PMC3596024/
[122] Ibid., Eva KW, Hatala RM, Leblanc VR, Brooks LR. Teaching from the clinical reasoning literature: combined reasoning strategies help novice diagnosticians overcome misleading information. Med Educ. 2007;41(12):1152–1158 [PubMed] [Google Scholar]
[123] Larry Dossey, MD. *Reinventing Medicine: Beyond Mind-Body to a New Era of Healing.* Harper Collins Publishers. 1999. Pg. 174.
[124] Michelle L. Castro, M.Ed. *What is Intuition and How Do I use it?* http://index-of.es/z0ro-Repository-3/Spirituality/intuition.pdf
[125] Scott D. Alison PhD. Psychology Today, *5 Surprising Ways that Heroes Improve our Lives.* Apr. 16, 2015. https://www.psychologytoday.com/us/blog/why-we-need-heroes/201404/5-surprising-ways-heroes-improve-our-lives#:~:text=People%20need%20heroes%20because%20heroes,and%20because%20heroes%20are%20inspiring.&text=Heroes%20elevate%20us%20emotionally%3B%20they,become%20heroes%20and%20help%20others.

[126] Ibid.
[127] Ibid.
[128] Ibid.
[129] Ibid.
[130] Ibid.
[131] Ibid.
[132] Ibid.
[133] Ibid
[134] Bill Moyers interview with Joseph Campbell. *Joseph Campbell and the Power of Myth.* June 21, 1988. Moyers on Democracy. https://billmoyers.com/content/ep-1-joseph-campbell-and-the-power-of-myth-the-hero%E2%80%99s-adventure-audio/
[135] www.QuantumHealingMagazine.com; Issue 11, April 2011
[136] Ibid.
[137] Ibid.
[138] Ibid.
[139] Ibid.
[140] *Biofeedback in Medical Practice.* US National Library of Medicine, National Institutes of Health. June 26, 2017 https://www.ncbi.nlm.nih.gov/pmc/articles/PMC2939454/
[141] Robert A. Nash, MD. *Common Sense Medicine – a Medical Doctor's Prescription for Health Care.* iUniverse, Inc. 2000. Pg. 174
[142] Wayne W Dyer. Harper Collins Publishers. Aug. 21, 2001 https://www.harpercollins.com/products/youll-see-it-when-you-believe-it-wayne-w-dyer?variant=32207787524130
[143] Alexandra Sifferlin, *The Healing Power of Nature.* July 14, 2016. Time.com. https://time.com/4405827/the-healing-power-of-nature/
[144] Ibid. Quoting Danielle Shanahan, University of Queensland, Australia
[145] Ibid. Quoting Yoshifumi Miyazaki, Chiba University, Japan.
[146] Ibid. Quoting Dr. Qing Li, Nippon Medical School, Tokyo
[147] Ibid.
[148] Ibid.
[149] Ibid. Quoting Proceedings of the National Academy of Sciences, 2015
[150] Ibid. Quoting Ming Kuo, University of Illinois at Urbana-Champaign

[151] Ibid. Quoting Paul Piff, University of California-Irvine.
[152] Allison Michelle Dienstman. "10 Unexpected Benefits of Spending Time in Nature." Goodnet.org. March 24, 2019. https://www.goodnet.org/articles/10-unexpected-benefits-spending-time-in-nature
[153] *Foods that Harm, Foods that Heal*. Reader's Digest Association, Pleasantville, New York, December 1997, pg. 74
[154] Ibid.
[155] *Foods that Harm, Foods that Heal*. Reader's Digest Association, Pleasantville, New York, December 1997, pg. 120
[156] https://www.arthritis-health.com/types/gout/what-are-purines
[157] https://www.health.harvard.edu/heart-health/potassium-rich-foods-linked-to-lower-stroke-risk-
[158] https://www.livescience.com/47696-potassium-may-lower-stroke-risk.html
[159] https://nccih.nih.gov/health/know-science/how-medications-supplements-interact?page=8
[160] https://www.ncbi.nlm.nih.gov/pmc/article/PMC5569602/
[161] Consumer Reports on Health, January 2007, pg. 10
[162] Ibid.
[163] Ibid.
[164] https://www.nccih.nih.gov/health/know-science/how-medications-supplements-interact/page-5
[165] *Foods that Harm Foods that Heal, an A-Z Guide to Safe and Healthy Eating*, Reader's Digest Association, Pleasantville NY/Montreal, pg. 226
[166] Ibid.
[167] https://www.uspharmacist.com/article/drug-interactions-with-vitamins-and-minerals; Maria Marzella Sulli, PharmD and Danielle C. Ezzo, PharmD, St. John's University College of Pharmacy and Allied Health Professions, Jan. 23, 2007
[168] Ibid

www.ingramcontent.com/pod-product-compliance
Lightning Source LLC
Chambersburg PA
CBHW071454040426
42444CB00008B/1334